LANCIA
DELTA

LANCIA DELTA

NIGEL TROW
PHOTOGRAPHY BY ANDRÉ MARZOLI

OSPREY
AUTOMOTIVE

HALF TITLE **Anatomy of the Group A Delta 4 × 4. Total traction, total dominance.**

TITLE PAGE **Lancia rallying began and ended with production cars. From Fulvia to Delta via Stratos and 037.**

Published in 1993 by Osprey Publishing,
Michelin House, 81 Fulham Road,
London SW3 6RB

A catalogue record for this book is available from the British Library.

ISBN 1-85532-239-0

Editor Shaun Barrington
Page design Colin Paine
Typeset by Tradespools Ltd, Frome, Somerset
Printed by BAS Printers Limited, Over Wallop, Hampshire

Contents

Acknowledgements

WRITING THIS BOOK has required the help and advice of various people and organisations. These include Dr. Paul Mayo, Lancia Motor Club Librarian; Tom Pleterski, Director of Public Relations at Lancia; Paolo Negro of the Italian Lancia Club; Hougette Boyagis, Fiat/Lancia UK; Centro Storico, Fiat; the Biscaretti di Ruffia Museum, Turin and Italdesign, Turin.

All of the sports photographs were taken by André Marzoli, who opened his entire and remarkably comprehensive archive to me. Other photographs were kindly provided by Lancia in Turin.

The technical specificiations are reproduced from the revised, second edition of *La Lancia* by kind permission of the author, Wim Oude Weernik and the publishers, Motor Racing Publications Ltd.

Dedication
In Memory of my friend Roger Perry, who died in 1991.

1   D is for Design

HAVING SPENT MUCH of their history building cars that were seldom like any other, Lancia fell into line with other manufacturers in 1979 and introduced the Delta. It was a real lurch toward the orthodox. Its predecessor, the wayward, beautiful Gamma, was as eccentric a car as anything that Lancia had ever built, and before it, in 1972, the Stratos had similarly demonstrated a fine disregard for such notions as market research, product evaluation and consumer preference. The Delta, however, put a stop to such caprice. By 1979, with Fiat fully in control and a reactionary decade ahead, it was to be commercial reality and saleable cars that dominated Lancia.

That, at least, was the intention: whether it could be achieved was another matter, for at Lancia what counted most was style. Within Fiat there had always been vague unease about such vanities. For many, style was an ephemeral concern and during the 1970's the contradiction was expressed in a struggle between populists and elitists, centralists and federalists. Given the sheer size of the company and the ambivalent relationship it seemed to have with its colonies, particularly Lancia and Ferrari, this was not surprising. In the early days of Fiat's ownership, Lancia appeared to be regarded as a federal state. It resisted centralisation and carried on much as before, albeit with steadily increased use of Fiat components in its cars. This policy reflected the aims of a takeover that had more than asset stripping in mind. Fiat recognised

Giugiaro's first sketches for the Delta showed a simple, two box car wholly in keeping with the company's contemporary commercial needs.

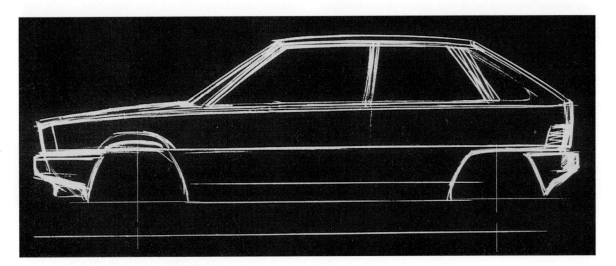

that a company like Lancia, an elder statesman of the Italian motoring establishment, was not sensibly shut down overnight, nor were its traditions to be carelessly discarded by the brutal introduction of new management, products and image. Hence the Stratos and the Gamma.

But could such freedom to be radical continue? By the late 70's the answer was becoming clear. Not if the marketing men had their way. No more Stratos', and certainly no more Gammas ought to be contemplated. Fiat intended to create a more neutral, less controversial image for Lancia, one that would increase sales and promote the marque to a new generation of conservatives with aspirations to dash.

By 1977 all the signs were clearly visible. Despite the total domination of world rallying by the Stratos, the project remained under pressure from those within Fiat (and Lancia, to an extent) who had never wanted to go exotic. What was needed, they believed, was the promotion of everyday cars and, as a consequence, Fiat's rally policy shifted in favour of the drab but successful 131 saloon.

Coincidentally, and perhaps inevitably, these same forces began to question the place of the specialist design studio. Did Fiat and its satellites really need big name designers for their workaday products? What, they asked, did Pininfarina, Bertone, Michelotti and Giugiaro do independently that could not be done in house? It was an old ques-

From the beginning the Delta presented an unostentatious exterior which reflected Lancia's traditions and the taste of its clients.

tion, one that arose from the conflicting claims of commerce, engineering and aesthetics. Before the age of the mass produced car, engineers held sway. Coachbuilders, artisans translated from carriages to motor cars, produced traditional forms, adapted by necessity and sometimes elaborated by art, with little sense of being in competition with engineers, whose development of the machine itself was unquestioned. One lot made chasses and the other lot dressed them up. Interestingly, it was Lancia who changed all that. The introduction of the Lambda in 1921, with its unitary body, marked the beginning of the end of such concord. Once the whole machine became an homogenous structure it fell entirely within the domain of engineering, a profession not all of whose members were much concerned with looks. The best, of course, included men of great visual sensibility, such as Lancia's own Battista Falchetto, of Lambda and Aprilia fame, and the aerodynamicist Jaray who, together with Dante Giacosa, designed the beautiful Fiat 508 Millemiglia. Most, however, believed form should follow function and if the form was commonplace, so be it.

In reaction to all this the flaccid practice of

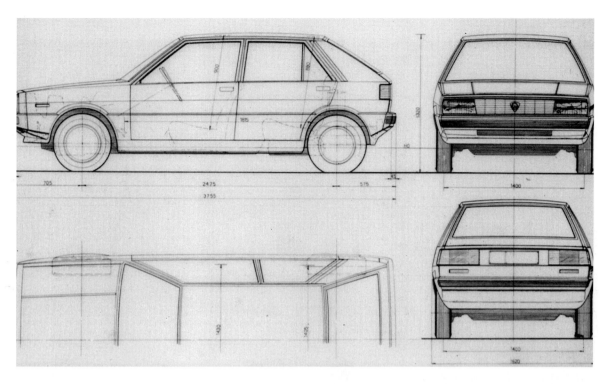

Rather than radical form, the Delta expressed radical intention in its bid to capture for Lancia a share of the medium size quality car market, dominated, in particular, by BMW. Angular, spare, there is nothing here to set the heart racing; but the Delta was never a concept car, it was a 'real' commodity as soon as Fiat earmarked the substantial development budget.

styling emerged. Particularly in the USA during the 1940's and 1950's, some dreadful confections were fettled, leading, in post-war Italy, to an almost puritan rebellion from such as Boano at Pininfarina. Of course, this is not to say that all American design of the period was ill founded. Raymond Loewy, a French industrial designer much influenced by the Bauhaus, was highly innovative and the work he did for the Studebaker Corporation, whose immediate post-war cars were shaped by him, was to have an enduring stylistic influence.

Yet Loewy, more than anyone, was ultimately responsible for the victory of styling over design. His association with big, mass production industries led to company executives grasping the notion of attractively styled products but without having the slightest interest or concern for the integrity or durability of the design. Styling was fashion: design for the throwaway world.

No effort of imagination is required to realise how little these attitudes found favour in Italy. In a country with so strong a visual and plastic tradition such indifference was unacceptable and no more complete a contrast could be found than that between Pinin Farina's Lancia B20 and Raymond Loewy's own later versions of the car, Blue Ray One and Two.

From the early 1950's to the mid 1980's Italian car body design flourished in the hands of indepen-

Lancia's normal practice, until the advent of the Delta, had been to design basic models in house. The involvement of Giugiaro in the project broke new ground for the Turin company.

dent houses who offered their original designs to manufacturers – to Lancia, Alfa, Maserati, Ferrari and to Fiat itself – for production. Each house, though open to the market, developed particular associations: Pininfarina was favoured by Lancia and Ferrari; Bertone made his name with Alfa and Maserati used Vigale, Touring and Ghia. All of these first-generation design firms, and others such as Zagato, found and trained the next generation of designers. Such was the success of these companies and their protégés that they eventually established production lines on which to realise their own designs, rather than handing them over for execution to manufacturing clients. It was just this expansion that inevitably prompted questions about whether in-house design and production might not be more profitable to corporations such as Fiat. It also promoted industrial recognition of that postmodern attitude whereby the object became feted rather than its creator.

Lancia, it should be said, had made a practice throughout their history of designing basic models in house. Many, such as the Aprilia and the Fulvia, had been remarkable and few of the design house variants ever improved upon the original concepts. However, the new view of how design should be used at Fiat brought with it the figure of the consultant and the most influential designer to benefit directly from this reappraisal was Giorgetto Giugiaro, a protege of Bertone and a design polymath. Giugiaro cut his teeth on cars and throughout the 1970's his Ital Design group produced outstanding designs for many major motor manufacturers. His work had considerable breadth and such fine machines as the Alfa Sud at one end of the scale, and the Maserati Merak at the other, came from his drawing board. What distinguished him particularly from many of his competitors was his view of design as a discriminating, intellectual process. This attitude led to the expansion of Ital Design into other, diverse fields ranging from men's fashion, to cameras, to graphics, to mosaics, pasta design, sewing machines, dish washers and all of the many disparate artefacts of modern industrial living. Such catholic awareness of the market was inevitably reflected back into car design and, in the case of the Delta, his first production design for Lancia and developed in close cooperation with their own engineers, he created a rational, habitable, stylish machine of quality.

Lancia turned to Giugiaro at a time when they desperately needed help. The late 1970's had not been good. The company had serious problems with build quality, an uneasy relationship with Fiat, an eccentric product range and nothing com-

Fiat decided to base the Delta on their own new car, the Ritmo, sold in Britain as the Strada. Lancia, with the mechanicals dictated to them, therefore needed a distinctive body to establish the car's identity.

petitive on the sporting front. The via Vincenzo Lancia was not a happy place.

With the advent of the Beta in 1972 – the product of a broken engagement between Citroen and Fiat – Lancia found themselves the inheritors of their own history in terms of the car's name, and international politics in respect of its French rear end. When Fiat bought them in 1968 Gianni Agnelli is reputed to have said 'Fiat with Lancia can never be stronger than Fiat without Lancia'. Thus damned, they had to take what came their way, which in this case happened to be one of the various joint developments undertaken by Fiat and Citroen during their courtship.

The Beta was a curate's egg. The good bits didn't do much to improve Lancia's image and the bad bits did considerable harm, particularly when they dissolved around the driver. Which was a shame, particularly since it harked back in name to a time when the infant Lancia company was beginning to establish its reputation for quality.

Despite the ups and downs of its history, Lancia's good name for quality and innovation was, however, so much a part of the Italian motoring psyche that Fiat, recognising its commercial value, allowed the company one last fling – the Gamma. Unfortunately, it was not a success. This final expression of Lancia eccentricity was a lovely car; it had fine road manners, a smooth, torquey engine, looked good, sounded good, was comfortable, elegant, sporty and unreliable. It did everything a car should do, but not for long. Although it remained in production for some eight years, the Gamma sold poorly and was Lancia's swansong as Lancia. From then on, Fiat heads would rule Lancia hearts. Which is how the Delta came about.

When the Fulvia finally ceased production in 1975, Lancia found themselves without a small quality car for the first time in over 40 years. The

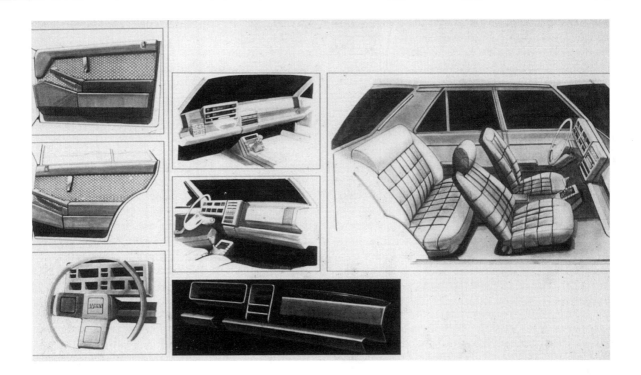

Giugiaro's particular concern as a designer was to produce a habitable motor car, where the greatest passenger space was achieved within the smallest shell. He was also concerned with quality and a sense of craftsmanship in the mass produced. Ital Design had proved its ability to produce that sense of additional quality for the lower end of the luxury market on several previous projects.

The original Delta project was called the Gamma. It then became the Epsilon, or Y5, but whatever the name Fiat invested heavily in it, earmarking some £150.000.000 to cover the long term development work.

tradition of little Lancias, begun in 1933 with the Augusta, had been steadily strengthened over the years by the Aprilia, Ardea, Appia and finally, 30 years later in 1963, the Fulvia. When production of this last, wonderful Lancia V4 ceased, belated thoughts of a replacement began to germinate, though initially without much effect. Beta production was steady and the newly introduced Gamma preoccupied many minds in the via Vincenzo Lancia. Little time was spared for thought on replacing the Fulvia.

Across Turin however, at Fiat, other plans were being made and other models being produced and of these one, the Ritmo, had particular significance for Lancia, since Fiat intended it to be the platform on which the Delta would be developed.

With the fundamental engineering already done, what Lancia needed was a body and an improved engine and Fiat,with good reason perhaps, brought in Giugiaro. Of course, facilities for this work were long established at the via Vincenzo Lancia. Until the Gamma, which was a Pininfarina design, the company had always created its basic body styles in

house and the studios were still operational at the factory, not yet having been absorbed into Centro Stile Fiat. And as far as the engineering went, Lancia were as good as any and better than most, despite the Gamma.

The Ritmo, sold in Britain and the USA as the Strada, came onto the market early in 1979. Coincidentally Lancia began to leak news of the Delta, code named Epsilon, and to release photographs of the car, whose form looked wholly developed and which ultimately proved to represent the production model accurately. In their basic outline, Ritmo and Delta had much in common. The Fiat, designed wholly by the Centro Stile, looked bulkier, although it was, in fact, slightly smaller in all dimensions. It was also fussier, with heavy, sharply defined plastic bumpers, thicker 'C' pillar and rounded front. Giugiaro did not use it as a pattern, though in many ways, given his brief to produce a luxurious four door, five seater within an overall length of 3750mm and with looks that would not frighten the children, certain similarities with the Fiat – and the Golf, the Horizon and the little Volvo – were inevitable. After all, the Delta was not intended as a concept car and since a two box solution was virtually mandatory, given the restricted length, the designer's options were quite strictly confined.

Perhaps it is a little unjust to deny the Delta any

conceptual qualities at all. It certainly lacked extravagance and ostentation, omissions wholly in keeping with Lancia tradition and much to the taste of the company's clients. Instead, rather than radical form, what it expressed was radical intention, for the marketing strategy was conceptually bold in demanding a small to medium sized car of a calibre and quality able to compete with BMW, Alfa, Saab and Volvo, but similar in size to the Golf, Ritmo and Alfa Sud and priced somewhere in between. These considerations consequently figured large in the choice of Giugiaro as design consultant. With Ital Design's well established reputation for giving a sense of craftsmanship to the mass produced and Giugiaro himself publicly expressing his concern for habitable motor cars, where the greatest passenger space was achieved within the smallest shell, the choice was obvious.

Lancia gave overall responsibility for the project to one of their directors, Sig. Rossiligno. Engineering they left in the capable hands of Ing. Sergio Camuffo, the company's Director of Research and Development. Both men were directly responsible to the Managing Director, Ing. Pier Ugo Gobbato, the power behind the pensioned-off Stratos, now displaced by Fiat's commonplace 131 Rally saloon. The Stratos, of course, was a Bertone design, which made the role of Giugiaro, as an ex-Bertone designer, somehow fitting in shaping the car which would ultimately carry on the Stratos tradition in the World Rally Championship.

Notions of the new car as a prospective world champion could not, however, have been uppermost in the minds of the designers as they got on with the task of preparing it for production. While one or two may have reflected on the fact that every post war Lancia, with the exception of the Gamma, had been used successfully in competitions of some sort or another, few would have given much for the chances of the restrained little saloon in the cockpit of international rallying. Not that it was intended to be tame. Given the market for which it was planned, high levels of performance as well as comfort were expected. A dull Lancia was a contradiction in terms for Fiat executives and Lancia designers alike.

When news of the latest Lancia began first to trickle out of the factory in 1978, it was accompanied by the expected PR hyperbole. The Epsilon, or Y5, was to banish criticism of Lancia quality once and for all. It would not corrode, since Saab had been persuaded to recite their rust repelling runes on Lancia's behalf; it would flatter customers with its comfort, excite them with its

exuberance and charm them with its discretion and manners. In short, it was being properly sold, something which Lancia, historically, had never been good at and for which they had paid the price.

Fiat invested much in the car's success. Something like £150,000,000 was earmarked for Lancia over the five years following its introduction and it was therefore to be expected that effective promotion figured large in the company's plans. The first publicity photographs to appear were carefully selected to show the car in full profile, emphasising its spare angularity and discouraging any suggestion that it was a badge-engineered Ritmo.

As announced, the Delta, which name soon replaced Epsilon (a letter too far, anyway, and cause for speculation about what the original Delta slot might have been reserved for) was offered with 1.4 and 1.5 engine sizes in the same package. These, of course, were a fraction of the displacement of Vincenzo Lancia's first Delta, the Tipo 56 of 1911. That car, named retrospectively when Lancia took up the Greek alphabet as a source of sequential names, had a whacking 4080cc side valve motor capable of developing some 55bhp at 1800rpm. Seventy years later its distant progeny produced 75bhp at 5800rpm from its 1300cc engine, which, in form at least, the namesakes had in common, since both powerplants were in line fours.

The 1979 Delta was a car of its time. Mechanically, the transverse engine reflected the usual space saving disposition common to all small, front wheel drive, post-Mini motor cars. Based on the iron block, alloy headed, single overhead camshaft Ritmo motor, the Lancia power unit was improved considerably by Camuffo's engineers, who, while retaining the Fiat's lower half and single, belt-driven overhead camshaft valve gear, extensively reworked the head internally. Although only minor power increments were made at first – up 10bhp on the Ritmo in both 1.3 and 1.5 litre form – the move to twin Webers, improved exhaust flow and, in the case of the larger engine, to breakerless electronic ignition, showed the direction the Delta project would take.

Similar refinement was evident in the suspension design. What was sought was the best compromise between comfort and handling. With this in mind, and also with an eye to costs, McPherson struts were employed all round. In outline the system once again reflected that of the Ritmo, but in detail it was markedly different. Various road testers had found the Fiat's performance less than good overall, noting particularly a lot of bump, thump and

wallow on irregular surfaces. This would not do for Lancia, whose engineers set about the problem of proper handling as if their good name depended on it; which, of course, it did.

Their first action was to throw out the transverse leaf spring used at the rear of the Ritmo. Such a device could be made to work in sophisticated cars like the Aprilia, but McPherson struts could not cope with the way such a spring disposed of its energies. Lancia therefore opted for coil springs all round, with those at the back well located by twin transverse links, picked up close to the centreline of the car, and single trailing links on either side to cope with brake reaction.

All four struts were encircled by their springs and firmly located, the front pair being carried on wide based wishbones and articulated at the top on roller thrust bearings, with those at the rear carried in rubber bushes. Rubber was used extensively throughout the system in pursuit of silence and compliance, made easier by long wheel travel – 170mm at the front and 220mm at the back – and an extended wheel base, with anti-roll bars front and rear to counteract undesirable side effects.

The braking system was conventional, with a

The production Delta was actually 100mm longer than its original design. Marketing considerations deemed Giugiaro's first compact designs too 'cosy' and the chassis engineers certainly did not complain about the longer wheelbase.

diagonally split circuit operating 226mm discs at the front and 186 drums at the back through a vacuum servo.

Five-speed gearboxes were fitted to both the 1.3 and 1.5 versions of the car, but with different ratios. Given the more sporting character of the 1500cc engine, close ratio 3rd and 4th gears were provided, with maximum speed attained in 5th. The 1300 car, conversely, while sharing common 1st and 2nd gear ratios with its larger sibling, had the three top ratios geared up, with 5th being an effective over-drive in the interest of good fuel economy.

This mechanical package, taken as a whole, represented a competent car but not a great one. No-one in Fiat or Lancia claimed anything out-standing for the Delta's dynamics, nor did they anticipate the Jeckyll and Hyde characteristics to be revealed in the future. What they were going for was style, quality and a specific market share. As

the luxury arm of Fiat's mass produced car manufacturing, Lancia managers knew that however tolerant the parent company had been in the past, the time had come to earn their keep in the corporation. In the longer term, Fiat recognised that Lancia's real value to them lay in the production of larger, executive cars, a domain where Fiat traditionally encountered market resistance. The beautiful but uncommercial Fiat 130 Coupe was past proof of this and the corporation's marketing experts well knew how to avoid similar mistakes in future. However, until a new, large, luxury Lancia appeared Vincenzo's old firm would have to prove its worth with a little one.

The sales targets established for the Delta were set at 200,000 units in 1980, an increase of 40% over previous achievements. Lancia estimated total European sales in the small to medium car market at some 4,000,000 in 1980, with a home market of 500,000. They anticipated Delta sales in Italy of around 80,000 cars with the rest going to export, though not to the USA or Japan. They also expected the market to grow by 40% annually.

With such tough objectives, Lancia had every

ABOVE **Effective ergonomics and instant data display formed a central part of the Ital group's vehicle design philosophy.**

RIGHT **The Delta's homologation file gives the original approval date as August 30th. 1979. It was to prove the longest lived Lancia ever.**

incentive to get the new car right, for competition in the market was fierce, with the car to beat the firmly established and admired Alfa Sud, well on the way to becoming a classic in its own time. Not that Lancia ever acknowledged the Sud as a direct competitor. In their eyes the larger Giulietta, the BMW 320, the Audi 80 and the Volvo 343 were the cars whose markets they wished to take. Nevertheless, so good was the little Alfa flat four that the Delta would inevitably be compared with it.

Giugiaro's design for the Delta body was clever. The initial concept, actually called the Gamma, was of a four door wedge with a long, comfortable wheelbase, an impertinent stub of a tail and a square short nose, its bumpers integral at both ends and the traditional Lancia shield sharp in the grille:

FIAT AUTO S.p.A.

TORINO

AUTOVEICOLO PER TRASPORTO PROMISCUO
*TIPO 831 AB0 (LANCIA DELTA 1300)

ANNO 1979

Omologato dal Ministero dei Trasporti - Direzione Generale M.C.T.C.
Certificato n. **19670 OM** in data **30 Agosto 1979**
È autorizzato il rilascio della dichiarazione di conformità
(3° comma art. 53 del T.U. 15-6-1959, n. 393)
(A richiesta può essere rilasciata la carta di circolazione per autovettura)

EDIZIONE 1984

Annulla e sostituisce il D.G.M. 405, Edizione 1982 e i successivi 5 fogli aggiuntivi di aggiornamento

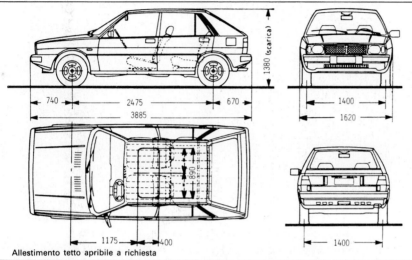

PUNZONATURA: vedere pagina 42.

Allestimento tetto apribile a richiesta

---

* **TIPO DELLA STRUTTURA:** .... scocca portante
Carrozzeria .... chiusa
Posti { sedile anteriore .... n.   2
       { totali .... »   5

DIMENSIONI:
Lunghezza max .... m   3,885
Larghezza max .... »   1,620
Altezza minima dal suolo (a carico) .... »   0,124
* Passo (a carico) .... »   2,475
Diametro minimo di volta .... » 10,610
* Carreggiata (a carico) { anteriore .... »   1,400
                          { posteriore .... »   1,400

PESI:
Tara: kg 955 + conducente kg 70 = ... kg 1025
Portata utile .... »   330
* Peso complessivo .... » 1355
* Peso rimorchiabile .... » 1025
* Peso max ammesso su asse { anteriore .... »   750
                            { posteriore ...... »   750

* **STERZO:** .... a sinistra oppure a destra

SOSPENSIONI:
Anteriore: a ruote indipendenti, con molle elicoidali e
montanti telescopici che incorporano gli am-
mortizzatori idraulici, barra stabilizzatrice.
Posteriore: a ruote indipendenti, con molle elicoidali e
montanti telescopici che incorporano gli am-
mortizzatori idraulici, barra stabilizzatrice.

RUOTE: { motrici .... anteriori
          { con cerchio .... 5B x 13

Pneumatici: { anteriori ....145 SR 13 oppure 165/70 SR 13
            { posteriori ..145 SR 13 oppure 165/70 SR 13

* **FRENI:** (vedere pagina 2).

MOTORE:
* Posizione .... anteriore
* Denominazione o Modello 831 A.000
* Funzionamento .... motore Otto

---

* Tempi .... n.   4
* Cilindri .... »   4
* Diametro cilindri .... mm 86,4
* Corsa .... »   55,5
Cilindrata totale .... cm³ 1301
Potenza fiscale CV   15
Rapporto di compressione   9,5
* Potenza massima (norme IGM) .... { CV   75
                                        { a giri/1' 5800
Coppia massima (norme IGM) .... { kgm 10,7
                                      { a giri/1' 3600
Raffreddamento .... a liquido, con pompa e radiatore

FRIZIONE: .... monodisco a secco

CAMBIO DI VELOCITÀ:
N. 4 marce in avanti e retromarcia.

Marce	Rapporti cambio	*Velocità calcolata a n. giri max potenza Rapporto finale pignone-corona 1 : 3,765		
		Pneumatici		
		145 SR 13	165/70 SR 13	
1ª	1 : 3,583	44,3	44,4	
2ª	1 : 2,235	71	71,2	
3ª	1 : 1,454	109	109,4	
4ª	1 : 1,042	152,1	152,7	
RM	1 : 3,714	42,7	42,9	

* **TRASMISSIONE:** .... meccanica
PRESTAZIONI:
1 km { partenza da fermo .... sec 38,1
     { lanciato .... »   23,3
Velocità max effettiva .... km/h 154,5
Consumo (norme CUNA): .... litri/100 km 8,57

IMPIANTO ELETTRICO:
Alternatore: .... Volt 12 Watt 600
Batteria: .... Volt 12 Ah 45
Dispositivi illuminazione e segnalamento: regolamentari.

SERBATOIO: capacità totale ....litri 45

SILENZIATORE: (vedere pagine 3 e 4)
Potenza specifica .... CV/t 73,2
Autoveicolo guidabile dai titolari di patente di categoria F
o B limitata.

---

* Caratteristiche essenziali la cui modifica comporta una nuova omologazione.

it was, to all intents and purposes, the final car. Of course, as the project emerged from the drawing board it was inevitable that detailed changes were made, not least to the overall length. Having carefully contrived a four door body capable of looking good on a wheelbase not much shorter than the car was long, Giugaro was a little peeved to be told to lengthen the design after a planning meeting had decided that it looked 'too cosy'. Nevertheless, good designer that he was, he added an extra 100mm and there the dimensions stayed.

At this stage, it now seems, several design opportunities were lost. The basic wedge – or, more pompously, the trapezoid – on which the car was based offered the chance to slightly dramatise the profile and, at the same time, improve rear headroom. This was a serious omission since one of the recurring criticisms of the interior was head banging by tall folks. The Alfa Sud, an earlier Giugiaro design, did not cause its occupants to suffer so. With 86cm of height between seat squab and roof against the 83cm of the Delta, Alfa passengers travelled more comfortably. How was so simple an error made? Visually and ergonomically the car would have gained much by raising the roofline towards the rear, as was demonstrated by the S4, which had a far more interesting profile. Why was it not done? One can only guess that Fiat conservatism lay behind it. Had more attention been paid to

The Delta was formally introduced at the Frankfurt Show in September 1979. As had often happened in the past, production difficulties and disputes at Fiat's Lingotto plant prevented an earlier launch.

ergonomics and less to the false aesthetics of a fancy trim and an architecturally 'soft' interior, – with advice being sought from a sofa manufacturer – the Delta would have been a better car.

But if the interior was self-indulgent, the exterior structure was not. Stung at last by criticism of their fabrication standards, both Fiat and Lancia invested heavily in vehicle durability and structural integrity. Not to put too fine a point on it, the problem was rust, or rather the publicity surrounding certain rusted cars. While some of this was justified much was not, for in fact the Turin company's products were no worse than many of their competitors. Citroen, Alfa, Peugeot, Renault, many Japanese and certainly most British cars of the period were all likely to rot in northern climates. The cause – of modern origin – was light steel pressings welded up to form closed corrosion chambers. That the problem was less marked in Scandinavian and German cars was a reflection of the more stringent climatic conditions in which these were habitually used and the greater caretaken to minimise the consequent damage.

But once the threat to sales was apparent, Fiat took steps to counteract it and the corrosion protection developed for both the Delta and the Ritmo was done in association with the Swedish company, Saab. From the earliest planning stage the body was designed to resist rust. Dick Ohlsson, Saab's body engineering manager is reported to have been adamant that 'It [was] not simply a case of protective finishes being applied afterwards'. With this in mind Lancia and Saab's engineers considered every joint and seam in the car to be a potential rust trap and closed them accordingly with structural adhesives and plastic sealer. All of the outer panels were either galvanised or treated with 'Zincrometal', a US process in which the sheet steel stock was first immersed in an aqueous solution of chromic acid and zinc powder in suspension. It was then heated to boiling point, where the solution deposited a 2 micron layer of zinc and chromium oxide on to the metal. After that a 12 microns of zinc-based primer was applied.

Following assembly and painting, the whole underside of the car was coated with a PVC layer and the enclosed box sections were sprayed in 'Crylagard', an anti-corrosion oil. After all that the Delta should have lasted for ever.

Despite the lack of rear headroom, Lancia put great emphasis on the habitable quality of the interior and Giugiaro went to considerable lengths to select sympathetic fabrics for the trim, including the headlining. He also devoted considerable care to designing the dashboard, instrumentation and controls. Instrument panels had been a preoccupation of his for years. On setting up Ital Styling, the precursor of Ital Design, in 1968, shortly after leaving Ghia, one of his first projects was the Bizzarini Manta. This vogueish, three a breast design had a rather dismal interior but later work, on such cars as the Bora, Sud and Sud Caimano, was admirable for its intelligence and subtlety. Initial designs for the Delta followed the 'data cylinder' concept used in the Caimano, and given further expression in the Audi 80 based, 'Asso di Picche' of 1973. Linear, 'bar' displays were also explored but the final solution, in which two rectangular consoles presented the driver with vehicle data in one and controls in the other, represented a compromise, using traditional dials and gauges set out in a radical, but wholly rational manner. Only the steering wheel let the concept down for, instead of adopting a single spoke design, similar to that of the Megagamma and proposed at the initial Delta design stage, a heavy, data obscuring cross bar was chosen. One suspects the hand of Lancia marketing.

Once the final package had passed all its committee stages the car received Fiat's blessing and by the summer of 1978 prototypes had been up and running for some time. Six months later, in the early part of 1979, news and pictures began to seep out of the factory. Curiously, these leaks in many cases anticipated the launch of the Ritmo/Strada, though whether they were intended as support or challenge is hard to say. They certainly emphasised the differences between the two cars.

The Delta was formally introduced at the Frankfurt show in September 1979. As had often happened in the past, production difficulties at the factory – this time at Fiat's Lingotto plant, not Lancia's at Chivasso – prevented an earlier debut. Originally, Lancia intended to get the production line started in May, with the car being launched in June and on the market in Italy by September. Alas, the plan was scuppered by an industrial dispute and the Delta started life three months overdue.

2 D is for Development

THE TEST OF any motor car's success is whether it sells profitably. Initially, this depends on advertising, public relations and the motoring press. Of these three perhaps the last, at first, is most significant and influential and the Delta, praise be, quickly got itself blessed by the pundits. In January 1980, to much trumpeting and muttering, it was voted 'Car of the Year' by an international jury of 52 motoring journalists. As a result, throughout Europe Lancia's various advertising agents and the company's own publicity people had a field day, particularly in Great Britain, where a couple of agencies appeared to vie with one another in writing off several examples of the new car.

Lancia undoubtedly needed the endorsement provided by the competition, a ruse dreamed up by Britain's *Telegraph* magazine in 1972 as a source of copy, and subsequently turned international in 1973 with the involvement of *Quattroruote* (Italy), *Autovisie* (Holland), *Stern* (Germany) *L'Equipe* (France) and *Vi Bilaegare* (Sweden). Taken at face value, the consensus reached by experienced motoring writers was influential amongst the buying public. Not surprisingly it was also valued by the winning manufacturers, though in the case of the Delta it may well have been Fiat who appreciated the accolade even more.

They were not in good shape, you see. After 80 years in business, during which time the company had voraciously consumed all of its Italian competitors with the exception of Alfa Romeo, Fiat, in the eyes of many commentators, was somewhat overweight. In manufacturing terms it produced too many different models – from Autobianchis to Ferraris – and the management was unable to cope properly with the diverse results of its corporate appetite. For too long it had adopted a laissez-faire attitude towards its satellites and this now had to be remedied. So it was that in January 1979 Fiat reformed its automobile manufacturing interests into a new corporation, Fiat Auto, which brought together Fiat, Lancia, Ferrari and Autobianchi under a single corporate management, of which the Delta was an early manifestation. Fiat Auto, therefore, had high hopes for the new car and their advertising managers, aware of its importance, put the publicity machine into overdrive.

Now it is one thing to say that a product is good, quite another to prove it over time. In the case of a motor car this is particularly so, for what is produced has to survive dynamic use and abuse for years, always in unpredictable circumstances and in the hands of drivers and mechanics whose competence may range from masterly to non-existent. It is a tribute to the manufacturer that any mass produced vehicle survives at all.

It is also to their credit that the expectation of the buying public in general, and the motoring press in particular, is so high. These expectations apply in all cars but, when a car is launched with laurels, they become especially pronounced. So it was with the Delta. From the road testing point of view, if it was Car of the Year, it had better prove it.

Not surprisingly, while the Italians lauded it, the British were sceptical, for the debacle of the Beta's rusted engine mounts was still news. This sorry episode coloured all reference to Lancia in the British press for years, despite the fact that the Company acted promptly and properly once the fault appeared in certain, though by no means all, Betas. The Delta, as a consequence, found itself very closely scrutinised.

The first appreciations of the car, published during 1979, were wholly derived from press handouts. *Quattroruote* came out with two pages in May and later in the year provided more detailed accounts based on short drives. These reports gave little real information about the car's performance, though they did offer the first, more or less disinterested view of its design, finish, interior and habitability.

On balance the car was well received, but not until November were *Quattroruote* testers able to give it a thorough physical. However, once they had hold of the Delta they measured it, examined its quality, checked out its comfort, its instru-

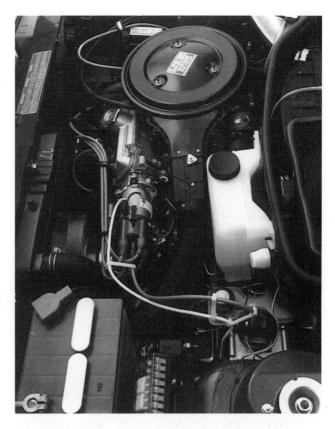

RIGHT **The clean, well designed under bonnet layout of the Delta 1300 characterised Lancia's approach to the whole car. When *Quattroruote* tested the 1.5 litre version they praised its power and general utility.**

BELOW **Cutaway drawings of the car revealed the Delta to be sturdy, compact and sensibly planned in all respects. What the drawings failed to show was the lack of rear headroom. In this respect it compared unfavourably with the Alfasud.**

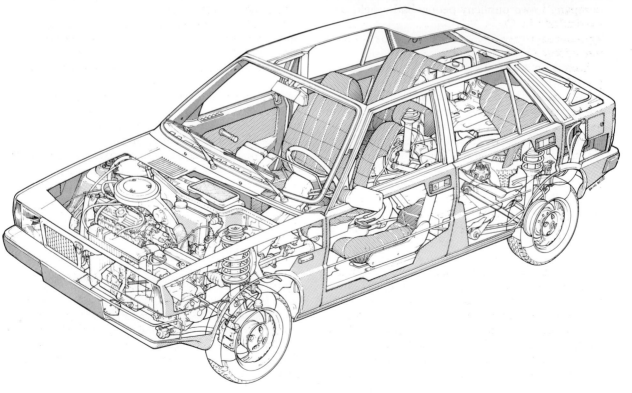

mentation, its ventilation, visibility, luggage space and the optional extras! Then they drove it, took performance figures and compared it with its rivals.

For this particular test the principal opposition consisted of Alfa Romeo's Sud and Giuletta, the Audi 80, the GS1220 Citroen, Fiat's Strada and 131, 1300, the Opel Kadett and Ascona 1.6, Peugeot's 305, Renault's 14, 18 and 20TL and the Volvo 343DL. In terms of maximum speed, the 1.5 Delta was quicker than all but the Alfa Giuletta 1.6 and 1.8, its 165kph being identical with that of the Sud ti 1.5. The acceleration tests from rest found the Alfas quickest, with the Delta fourth fastest. However, the fourth gear acceleration was only a little above the average for the group. Fuel consumption figures were not good. At 8.5L/100Km at 110kph the Delta was low in the ranking, though at the higher speed of 140kph it suddenly improved, moving up to third best with a figure of 11.2 L/100Km.

ABOVE **Soon after its launch the Delta was voted 'Car of the Year' by an international panel of motoring journalists. As a consequence it was very closely scrutinized by the motoring magazines. In general it was well received and there were few complaints about its carrying capacity.**

ABOVE RIGHT **McPherson struts, wide base lower wishbones and rack and pinion steering had been standard Lancia/Fiat practice for years. It performed well enough in the Delta but had none of the novelty of Lancia's long dead sliding pillars.**

RIGHT **Based on the traditional Fiat in line 4, sohc engine used in the Ritmo, the Delta engine was an extensive rework of the old design by Lancia's Ing. Camuffo and colleagues. Power went up 10 bhp at first.**

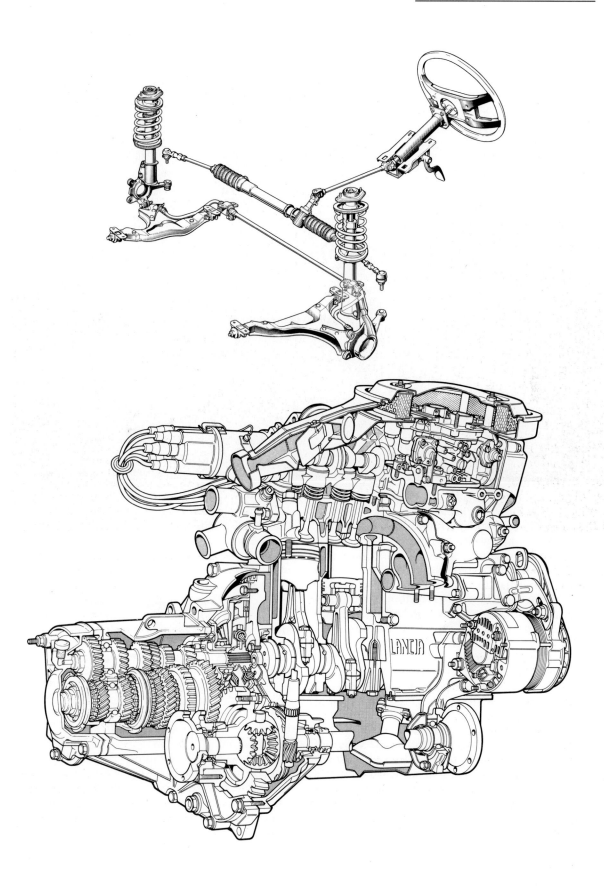

On the road the testers liked the car's road holding, its sporting character and the interior finish: they disliked its comparatively high price, its lack of headroom and the motor, which they found harsh and noisier than expected. Nevertheless, these criticisms did not mar their general enjoyment. The car sparkled on the road, doing everything expected of a Lancia and leading to the conclusion that, with time, it would repay Fiat's investment.

The first serious tests by British magazines appeared towards the back end of 1980. John Bolster took a Delta to Paris for *Autosport* and, on the whole, enjoyed the car, finding it sprightly and nimble, albeit at the cost of high fuel consumption.

John Thorpe, writing for *Motor*, was more circumspect. Thorpe had his Delta 1500 from new and ran it for seven months through the winter of 1980/81. He appeared to have had a thoroughgoing love-hate relationship with the car, liking its dynamic qualities and, interestingly, its finish. What annoyed him was the car's slipshod assembly, poor pre-delivery checks, incompetent service from agents and the familiar story of no

Model development began in 1982 with the introduction of the LX, an upmarket version of the Delta which came with split rear seats as standard, alloy wheels, metallic paint and three more horses. An automatic was introduced in the same year.

spares and high prices. Yet despite the many frustrations of living with the car, which, it should be added, were identical to those encountered in Italy by *Quattroruote* on a similar extended test, he liked it, finding that its motor, suspension, handling and ride more than overcame the frustrations caused by the carelessness of others. What he suspected was that the Delta was a good car with a better one trying to get out.

Taken as a whole the initial press reactions, and those of the public, whose opinions filtered back through the correspondence pages of the various magazines, was that Lancia had produced a pleasant, well-intentioned car, capable of meeting modern driving needs and with potential for further development. Which was, of course, precisely what Lancia and Fiat had in mind.

Traditionally Lancias have always started discreetly, only flexing their muscles as time passed. New models were usually introduced with small capacity engines set in exemplary chassis, capable of chewing whatever was bitten off later. The Delta, in this respect, was typical; what was different and challenging, however, was the nature and extent of technological change in the motoring air at the time of its appearance. For the threats to fuel supplies, which emerged in the 1970's, led to pressures for improved economy, coupled with performance and stability. This, in time, resulted in radical revision in vehicle design, revisions with which the Delta would have to contend.

In so many respects it seemed that the car's designers were oblivious to change. Weight reduction and aerodynamics, for example, were apparently overlooked as significant factors influencing efficiency, omissions made the more surprising by Lancia's long involvement with motor sport. Indeed, at the Borgo San Paolo workshops, just around the corner from the Lancia skyscraper, and also across Turin at Abarth, in the Corso Marche, was all the knowledge and experience necessary to produce a better car, yet it was seemingly ignored.

It is hard to know why this was, for the signs were there for all to see. In 1980 the hot issues were publicly expressed by manufacturers such as Audi, who with their stunning five cylinder, four wheel drive Quattro, were soon to be as dominant in world rallying as Lancia and the Stratos had been five years earlier. And on a more mundane level, manufacturers everywhere pursued research into fuel and ignition systems, the use of turbochargers for both petrol and diesel engines, plastic body parts and other weight reducing devices, wind tunnel studies aimed at shapes with low drag coefficients and tyre research intended to lessen the amount of power lost at the point of contact with the road.

Of course, many of the innovations resulting from this work could be 'bolted on', as it were. Fiat, naturally, were as involved in research as any and the Delta was quite capable of being adapted. Indeed, as time passed it came to reflect many of the advances heralded in 1980 except, unfortunately, shape and weight, for the coefficient of friction between research and marketing, once established, is never easily reduced.

The first changes appeared early in 1982. After a necessary period of consolidation in which production bugs were squashed and the car was slotted into its market niche, an upmarket version, the LX,

and an automatic were introduced. Neither was radically different from the initial model. The LX1500 and 1300 both offered more refined interiors, with split rear seats as standard, rather than options. They also came with metallic paint, alloy wheels, heated screens, electric windows and, for the 1300, an extra 3bhp.

The automatic Delta, announced in May, used an Automotive Products three speed torque converter gearbox built in Verona. Lancia had made plain their intention to include such a version in the range when they issued their first press releases, and the choice of the AP design, which was similar to that of the Beta, was in keeping with the Delta's conservative image. While this was understandable in some ways, a case might have been made for making use of the Van Doorne Transmatic, in which Fiat had a financial stake and was actively developing. The case was strong on grounds of economy, for the automatic Delta, as produced, was even less fuel-efficient than the manual versions, which had won no prizes for conservation from any of its testers. The Van Doorne/Fiat box, on the other hand, was proving to be as economical on the road as the manual Strada in which it was tested.

Fiat invested considerable amounts of money and time in Transmatic development. The new gearbox was a replacement for the old, familiar Variomatic used in the Daf car by Van Doorne, its parent company, prior to selling the Dutch car plant to Volvo. After the sale, Van Doorne sought new partners with whom to continue their automatic transmission developments and, ultimately, a new company was set up with Fiat, Borg Warner and the Dutch government as co-owners.

From 1974 much original research was undertaken in Italy, with Fiat 128's and then Ritmos being used as test beds. The Transmatic design, though expensive to build, satisfied most of the engineering criteria, particularly in its extended torque capacity. The earlier Variomatic system, which used fabric-and-rubber belts, had limited torque capacity, but in the new design this was overcome by transmitting force in thrust, through several hundred small trapezoidal steel plates, each slotted into steel guide belts, rather than belts in tension, as in the older design. The result, in practice, was a short, compact gear box with a wide ratio spread, capable of returning fuel consumption figures every bit as good as its manual counterpart. In this respect alone it could have been useful to Lancia.

The first genuinely interesting innovation to appear was the four wheel drive turbo, the Delta

4X4, introduced in the Spring of 1982 at the La Mandria test track outside Turin. At last, after three years, the Delta was beginning to evolve. The La Mandria tests were interesting and portentous. A surprisingly well finished Delta, looking virtually identical to the standard car but for a deep front spoiler and Delta Turbo 4X4 emblazoned on its flanks, was presented to invited journalists. Initially it was demonstrated by works drivers but later in the day the prototype 4X4 was made more generally available. The car, which suffered a certain instability, generated the inevitable speculation about the company's intentions and then fell out of the news until it reappeared at the Turin show some months later.

Lancia's achievement in getting the 4X4 to La Mandria and public display was considerable. The project had begun barely twelve months earlier, no doubt prompted by Audi and Peugeot activity. Much of the development, which included a twin-engined Trevi devised by Giorgio Pianta, was done in collaboration with Ital Design, who had earlier demonstrated their engineering competence by producing a 4X4 Fiat Panda. The system adopted

The first major increase in engine size saw the introduction of the 1500, closely followed at the end of 1982 by the 1600 GT. This car gave buyers a first taste of what was to come, for with 105 bhp and 175kph it was quick and comfortable.

for the Delta owed much to this work.

But the prototype offered more than four wheel drive. Tucked under the bonnet, in place of the standard 85bhp 1.5 engine was a 1600cc twin cam Beta unit, its power boosted to 130bhp at 5600rpm by a Garrett type turbo. This engine, together with the new transmission, transformed the previously rather staid Delta into a most potent performer.

The drive system itself was characterised by a third, torque separator differential, built into the original five speed, front drive gear box. This was accomplished with little difficulty, in terms of dimension, and its function was to divide the torque between the front and rear axles through an epicyclic gear train. The major part of the power, 58%, was transmitted to the front wheels with the balance of 42% going to the rear. If, however, one set of wheels lost grip, the separator could be locked out manually and power transmitted to either front or rear through the now directly connected front and rear differentials.

A split propeller shaft, carried in a light centre bearing, took the drive to the rear differential, which was mounted on the body on reinforced cross members. The rear suspension remained unaltered, retaining the familiar McPherson struts with widely based transverse arms, positive longitudinal location and an anti roll bar. A larger clutch was fitted and the final drive ratio was changed to 3.583:1 from the standard Delta's 3.765:1.

Turbocharged engines were not new to Lancia. They had gained experience in the field with the Stratos – though with sometimes disastrous consequences – and since 1979 had been campaigning the Beta Monte Carlo Turbo as a Group 5 endurance racer. The principal lessons learned about turbos by Lancia's race engineers concerned cool-

With the 1982 cars came new interiors, which added considerably to the sense of luxury sought by Lancia in the efforts to promote the Delta.

ing. In the early days several Stratos Turbos caught fire and subsequent Monte Carlo Group 5 engine developments had centred on temperature reduction throughout the system. As a result, much data was available to the team working on the Delta 4X4, which was given a bigger radiator and electric fan, a heat exchanger in the oil circuit and a further heat exchanger to cool the air from the turbocharger before supplying it to the carburettors. An additional air duct was also provided at the back of the engine to direct cooling air onto the turbo itself. Taken together, engine and transmission provided a fast and intriguing combination with which Lancia's Delta might make the mark planned for it.

Ever cautious, however, Lancia introduced the 1.6 engine *sans* turbo, in the first instance, announcing as they did so their intention to quickly follow up with an HF Turbo version and then the production 4X4. The GT, as the 1600 was called, was made available in Italy at the end of 1982. Although little different in outline from Giugiaro's original design, the body had been subtly reshaped in an effort to reduce drag and given a mild facelift by reducing its chrome and introducing fashionable black surrounds to the glass. Although small,

these changes altered the presence of the car. With its re-profiled, full width front spoiler, a small, discreet lip to the rear of the roof, pretty, 14-in alloy wheels carrying Pirelli P8/65 low rolling resistance tyres and lighter plastic bumpers, the latest Delta looked extremely purposeful. Not that Lancia were, even then, making great play for a sporting reputation. They might have given the GT a 105bhp engine, discs all round, 175kph and acceleration to match, but they were still concentrating on comfort, finish and habitability as the car's principal selling points.

Quality continued to preoccupy the Lancia management; beating the reputation for carelessness which had grown up around the marque had become something of an obsession. In the early 1980's Fiat were pouring millions into the company to support this effort and in reality the investment was beginning to pay off. When the GT was introduced, Lancia's sales in Italy and abroad were slowly increasing, owing in large part to the growing popularity of the Delta. New cars were in the pipeline, with the rumour mill beginning to leak news of a three box model, the Prisma; a luxury mini, the Y10 and a new, two litre Lancia diesel engine. Much production PR was also landing on journalists' desks. Vittoria Ghidella, Fiat's chief executive and general manager, let it be known that the £60m already spent on reshaping Lancia's production facilities was proving a good investment. He also felt that the destructive labour relations that had so damaged Lancia in the 1970's were now a thing of the past. 'Lancia made good cars', he said, 'but manufacturing control was poor. Fiat have put that right while still maintaining Lancia's uniqueness.'

Giugiaro's obsession with dashboard design continued as the Delta evolved. Although retaining the two block concept, in which instrumentation was grouped in one console and controls in another, presentation (and steering wheel design) were subtly changed.

LX, GTie and HF Turbo – a range spanning trio covering the Delta's long and successful life. Such steady development of simple beginnings is characteristic of Lancia.

In Britain, however, Fiat gave up the struggle to sell Lancias and passed the national concessions to a Heron Group company, the rather unimaginatively named Lancar. Although a target of 10% of national sales had been set for the Italians, aspirations for the British market were merely to improve on the total of 5,200 cars sold in 1982. To meet these goals, further improvements in quality were obviously essential. Despite all claims to have solved build and corrosion problems there were still too many complaints from customers about poor assembly and also, sadly, of rust. That this particular problem should still occur when so

much had been invested in its prevention, was infuriating to Lancia management. It could only be the result of carelessness and the company's personnel managers redoubled their efforts in an attempt to get the work force to take some pride in the cars they built. After all, in the days of the Lancia family there had been immense loyalty from all who worked for Vincenzo. The quality of the cars built then was still part of the mystique of the marque and, as such, was not to be carelessly abandoned. Unfortunately, times had changed and the company was driven to various morale boosting strategies, such as posters along the production line showing a variety of national flags, including the Union Jack, which asked; 'Is your quality as good as theirs?'

Of course, one of the contributory factors adversely affecting quality was the largely manual production line at the Chivasso factory. Fiat's investment in robotic assembly had not spread to

Lancia, where human failing still undermined management's best intentions. However, as time passed, the problems were solved. The Chivasso director, Alberto Pianta, set high standards, making the best use possible of computerised systems of quality and stock control, and his efforts to improve build quality were reflected in the LX and GT models.

Lancia was now at the beginning of a slow recovery from the troubles of the late 1970's. The Delta was established and the introduction of the 1600GT proved extremely popular. It was therefore an appropriate time for the range to expand with the announcement of the Prisma, a sort of three box super Delta designed, once again, by Giugiaro. This latest Lancia, which followed the big boot trend set by the Trevi within the Beta range, used a detuned 1600 GT engine, its power reduced and softened but still providing a useful 100bhp.

Other engine developments were also taking place and at the time of the Prisma's introduction a clutch of Deltas were running around Turin powered by new, 2 litre diesel engines. These cars, with 65bhp available, had a performance similar to that of the standard petrol driven 1300 Delta but with better fuel consumption. Their Lampredi-designed engines, which were intended for the Prisma, were too tall for the Delta and the prototypes were identified by a bulge in the bonnet and Prisma grille and headlights. They looked good.

Although this was to be Lancia's first diesel-engined car, the technology was by no means new to the company. Right from the beginning, Vincenzo Lancia had been as interested in commercials as in passenger cars and for some thirty-five years, until Fiat killed Lancia's trucks and buses in 1972, diesel engines, some with turbos, were in regular production.

However, putting a diesel in a Delta did not mean Lancia were abandoning their sporting image. Diesel-engined saloons had their place but of greater significance to the Delta's career, and certainly of interest to the younger end of the Lancia market, was the 1600 Turbo, launched complete with the prestigious HF title, a volatile 130bhp and a genuine 200kph. For the first time, the Delta looked like a real successor to the Fulvia: and with a bit more attention it might even outdo the Stratos.

3 Supercharging and Saloons

DURING 1984 LANCIA consolidated the Delta range, which now comprised five models and catered for all tastes. From the single cam 1300 through to the twin cam 1600GT and HF Turbo, with manual and automatic transmissions available and an excellent diesel saloon in the Prisma, the company found itself with a good production base and rising sales.

These improving prospects carried with them a restatement of Lancia's traditional sporting image.

Although quite clearly a saloon, the Delta's two box shape did not appeal to all of Lancia's potential customers and in 1983 the arrival of the booted Prisma extended the market to those who liked to keep their luggage in its place.

Since 1976, when the Fulvia ceased production and the Stratos won the last of its hat trick of World Rally Championships, that image had faded, largely as a consequence of Fiat politics. For several years Lancia had been required to concentrate their competition efforts on endurance racing, leaving international rallying to Fiat and the successful but unglamourous 131, with which they won the World Championship in 1977, '78 and '80.

Lancia, on unfamiliar ground, achieved less. The Beta Monte Carlo Turbo, introduced in 1978, was a brave venture. It did much to keep endurance racing alive in the doldrums of the late 1970's and in 1980, helped by the clever tactics of team manager Cesare Fiorio, gave Lancia the World Cham-

ABOVE **The first petrol engined Prismas were offered with 1300, 1500 and 1600cc engines. Although Lancia claimed that they were quite distinct from the Delta, they were about as different as a tabby from a Manx cat.**

BELOW **The Prisma Diesel marked a major change in Lancia history. Although the company had built commercial diesels for decades, this was the first time they had used compression ignition in a passenger car.**

pionship. But despite this success it was not a great car, for neither it nor its successors, the LC1 and LC2, could really cope with Porsche. It was also the case that endurance racing was perhaps the least popular part of motor sport. As a consequence, Lancia gained little publicity from its often expensive efforts.

But in 1983 the picture changed. Using a new car, the Rally Abarth, code named 037, Lancia became World Rally Champions once more and their star began to shine again.

For homologation purposes they produced a small number of these 037's in road form. Lancia therefore had an exotic, high performance car back in their model range for the first time since 1975. In commercial terms, however, it was obviously insignificant. The price was high, few were made and few bought. Much more important was the HF Delta and this car, backed by the company's successful return to World Championship Rallying, was the one that counted on the balance sheet.

The 1.6 HF Turbo Delta was Lancia's quickest

The 1.6 HF Turbo. Although indistinguishable at a glance from its predecessors, the HF Turbo was another thing altogether. It was a fast, exciting and essentially civilised car, depending upon one's definition of civilisation.

mass production car yet built. It also represented a significant technological decision in moving to turbocharging after a brief flirtation with the older supercharged system of forced induction. Never hasty in such matters, Lancia's engineers trod a cautious path towards the turbo. Their initial decision to develop the Volumex supercharger for use on the Beta Coupe and HPE was based on production issues and on image. The supercharger, with its constant pressure, made for smoother driving. It was also easily adapted to existing engines which, in 2 litre form, acquired the performance of 2.5 litre engines without putting the manufacturer to the vast expense of retooling.

Supercharging fitted Lancia's image. In an odd sort of way the reversion to an earlier technology in the face of a universal move towards the turbo was characteristic. A Lancia, even a Fiatized one, could never be quite like any other car and the company's engineers seldom seemed to set out to solve a problem from the same starting point as anyone else. In the case of the Volumex supercharger, this open-minded inventiveness was encouraged by a powerful engineer elsewhere in the Fiat group. Aurelio Lampredi, a great and sometimes misunderstood engine designer, responsible for, among other projects, the Squalo Ferrari and the production version of the Dino 246 engine, supported

supercharging. From his base at Abarth, Lampredi gave considerable assistance to Carlo Pangallo, one of Lancia's senior engineers and the man responsible for the Volumex and for the subsequent development of the Delta Turbo.

Pangallo had been with Lancia for many years and consequently possessed a sound understanding of the company's underlying identity. In an informative interview given to the British journalist Martin Sharp at the time of the Delta Turbo's introduction, he described the emergence of the new car's forced induction system. Plainly, from the conversation, both the Volumex supercharger and the first generation turbo were seen as interim steps towards more sophisticated high performance Lancia engines. In each case, however, the starting point was the venerable Fiat twin cam which, in the Delta, displaced 1585cc and was boosted by the widely used Garrett T3 turbocharger fitted with a diaphragm operated wastegate, set to blow at about 8 p.s.i.

Pangallo chose this set up largely for commercial reasons. As an engineer he preferred the KKK turbo, similar to that used by the racing department on the Monte Carlo Turbo endurance car

but, as he explained, while the poppet valve wastegate on the KKK was far superior to the Garrett, it was also far more expensive. What was justified for a few racing cars could not be afforded on the production line, whatever the engineering niceties.

Coping with the additional mechanical stresses imposed by a turbocharged regime led to significant internal changes to the Delta engine. An immediate need was to reduce the unblown engine's 9.35:1 compression ratio, which, by fitting pistons with shallow crowns and molybdenum rings, was reduced to 8:1. Gas temperatures also had to be lowered. This was achieved by installing an air-to-air intercooler, thermostatically set to open when intake air temperatures rose above 65°C. Since the laboratory tests showed full throttle air temperatures of some 120°C between the turbo and the intercooler, a sharp reduction was obviously necessary before that air reached the sealed twin

The first HF engines used Weber carburettors but the definitive version, shown here, made use of Bosch fuel injection. It was a wonderful engine, perhaps the high point of Fiat twin cam technology.

ABOVE **HF – the fastest five door hatch on the road.
190kph, a fine chassis, excellent acceleration,
comfort (of the firm kind) and nicely
understated style. Truly a child born at the right
time.**

BELOW **At the other end of the scale, the Prisma
Diesel Turbo offered economy, performance,
space and a little more dignity. This was a solid,
though by no means unexciting car designed for
those with no need to overtake everything in sight.**

Although the Prisma retained the wheelbase of the Delta, its overall length was increased by 295mm. Weight, however, did not increase markedly and the petrol engined 1600 was actually 25kgs lighter than the HF Delta.

Giugiaro's transformation of the Delta into a
Prisma involved a clever frontal facelift as well as
the addition of a boot. A little rake to the grille
and a few other minor cosmetic changes
wrought wonders.

choke Weber carburettor feeding fuel to the engine.

Retaining a similar carburettor to that used in the 1600GT Delta rather than moving to fuel injection was another instance of economics leading design, albeit temporarily. Pangallo explained that while his team acknowledged that injection would give more power, he had to balance the fact against the extra development time and retooling costs involved in moving away from carburettor induction. He had also to take account of the Bosch factor, for injection development would be a joint venture with the German firm, who were not noted for their flexibility. Then there was the electronic engine management system. The HF Turbo used the latest Magnetti Marelli Microplex system, with 16 pre-programmed advance curves feeding information to a control box. The Bosch injection system was incompatible with the Microplex, which

was yet another reason for staying with the carburettor.

Electronic engine management was essential to the efficiency of the Turbo engine. With its higher temperatures and pressures, necessitating sodium cooled stainless steel exhaust valves, stainless steel exhaust manifolds and stainless inserts in the head gasket, the need for precise ignition control was of paramount importance. The HF consequently incorporated the very latest technology from Magnetti Marelli.

Like the Digiplex, Marelli's previous control system widely used by such as Ferrari, the Microplex

BELOW **Forced induction at Lancia was largely in the hands of Ing. Carlo Pangallo. Despite their reintroduction of supercharging for the Beta, Delta blowing was left to the turbo for a variety of reasons.**

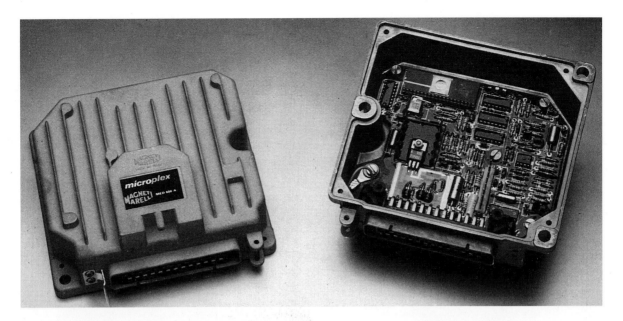

ABOVE **Delta blackbox. Like most turbos, Lancia's HF required sophisticated electronic engine management. This was provided by the Marelli Microplex, shown here with its lid off.**

RIGHT **How it works – ignoring, of course the complexities of microprocessor control of all functions. Turbocharging is a simple engineering concept: the fiendish trick is in optimising operations at each stage.**

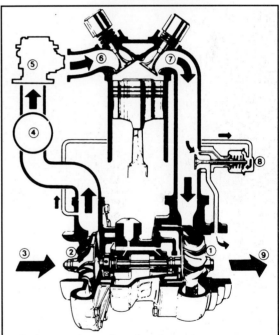

Schematics of turbocharging

1) Exhaust gas turbine
2) Turbocharger
3) Environment air
4) Air-to-air heat exchanger
5) Carburettor
6) Overpressure mixture
7) Exhaust gas
8) Waste-gate
9) Exhaust gas

control box was microprocessor driven. However, it went further than the eight curve Digiplex in being able to analyse considerably more data derived from sensors reading pressures, vacuum, temperature, engine speed and detonation characteristics. In this way engine performance, fuel use and exhaust emissions were kept at their optimum.

When the new car reached the press it was enthusiastically welcomed. Both Italian and English writers recognised its capacity to move the Delta out of the every day into that special category of understated high performance cars characteristic of Lancia. Although indistinguishable at a glance from its predecessors, the HF Turbo was a wholly different car and all who drove it were impressed. Well, most

were. Mike McCarthy, writing in *Autosport*, was not entirely convinced. He liked the engine and the chassis but referred to the car's heavy steering, poor gear change, lack of low speed performance and various other minor irritations. He said it was good when good but horrid when bad.

His was a lone voice, however. The HF earned yards of coverage throughout Europe and for the most part journalists liked it. Lancia presented the car as the fastest five door hatchback in its class. a claim that was indisputable: the Delta Turbo was the *only* five door hatch. All of its competitors – the Golf GTi, Astra GTE and Escort XR3i – were three door cars. Nevertheless, the HF was commendably fast, capable of over 190kph and with acceleration figures that averaged around 9 secs to 100kph.

Top speed was not, however, the car's real strength. Like most Lancias before it, the HF

HF dash, with sporty wheel, more engine information and lots more buttons. Interestingly, turbo data was banished from the instrumentation console.

scored in its handling. A good basic chassis, retuned to cope with the extra power of the turbo engine and fitted with Michelin's excellent new TRX asymmetric tread tyres made it primarily a driver's car. Out of town, on motorways or cross country, on dry or wet roads of varying surface, the HF proved to be quick and safe. Pushed hard into a corner it went into a mild understeer that could be killed by lifting off momentarily. When new and tight it demonstrated little, if any, signs of torque steer, despite its power. However, once wear set in this benevolence vanished and an HF with tired suspension could give its driver quite a fright.

Both the Delta (top) and the Prisma (bottom) received further attention to interior detailing and trim during the mid 80's. Marginally better rear head and legroom was provided in both cars, though the Prisma driver had less room than the pilot of a Delta.

Lancias have never been forgiving of poor maintenance. Despite its mixed parentage the Delta, once it moved into the ranks of the high performance car, proved just as demanding as the Gamma, the Stratos, the Fulvias, Flaminias, Aurelias and all of the other quirky cars produced by Lancia in its pre-Fiat days. Engineering nicety was not often compromised by the fact that it might be difficult to sustain out in the real world. As long as mechanics were well trained, garages had the right equipment and owners were fastidious, all would be well. Let one link break and the machine would suffer. The Delta, once it acquired a turbocharger, moved up to join its predecessors in that domain where faults could not be masked for long. And in the future, when the brilliant, complex Integrale would appear, the matter of precision maintenance was to become crucial.

Although plans for four wheel drive production cars were well advanced at Lancia in 1984, and Fiat were even preparing their lowly Panda to receive such a system, the real news on that front lay in another part of Turin, at Abarth's Corso Marche factory where the competitions department had its headquarters. Here great things were being planned. Meantime, back at the Via Vincenzo Lancia, Delta development stepped aside a while to be overshadowed by the little Y10 and more significantly by the Thema, Lancia's new flagship, conceived as a joint Lancia, Fiat, Alfa venture. In yet another of those Italian waltzes orchestrated by Fiat, where partners flirt with one another as they change, these grand families negotiated a trial *ménage à trois*. Out of discreet contacts and assignments which had been taking place since 1980, following negotiations by Fiat with Saab, for whom they harboured an ill-concealed passion, came potentially fruitful co-operation.

What was planned was sensible. None of the parties wanted to produce a single, corporate design. An 'Alfilia', or even perhaps a 'Fisaalla' would take centralism too far. Instead, motivated by economics, they intended a range of distinct cars, each reflecting the characteristics of its badge but using many common components. What finally emerged were cars with a shared floor pan clothed in different bodies and with different engines.

For Lancia, the need to provide a new top-of-the-range model to replace the Gamma had been pressing since 1980, when the Y9 project began. This design became joined to Fiat's Tipo 4 and Alfa's 154/156 proposals in preparing the way for an entirely new generation of two to three litre cars. Lancia's initial choice of engine for the Y9 was the ubiquitous PRV6, the single overhead camshaft V6 found in the larger Peugeot, Renault and Volvo cars. Fiat, ever sensible, chose to remain faithful to their long life twin cam four, however, and this engine, suitably embellished with fuel injection and turbocharging inevitably became a Lancia option in the Thema and, later, the Delta, where it performed with devastating effect. Alfa used its V6.

The arrival of the booted Prisma also diverted attention from the Delta. Lancia began the practice of turning successful two volume cars into three box designs back in the mid 1950's, when they transformed the neat little 1st series Appia into an ugly duckling by sticking on a luggage trunk and calling it the 2nd series. In the late 1970's they repeated the trick by turning the Beta into the even uglier Trevi, and now it was the turn of the Delta to grow a tail.

When the car first appeared in Italy in 1983 Lancia were at pains to point out that it was not a modified Delta but a wholly new design. Well they would, wouldn't they!

Everything new has to be very new in the great sales race. Not that such claims mattered much. Just as a wig and a moustache can change a man's appearance, so a box on the back and a new, sloping front end put an entirely new face on the Delta cum Prisma without changing much underneath. In a number of simple, clever moves, Giugiaro, who handled the transformation, turned the youthful Delta into a middle-aged saloon with pleasant and entirely inoffensive lines. Lancia were now in a position to appeal to those who preferred their baggage to know its place.

The Prisma proved a perfectly good and popular car. It was offered initially in 1300, 1500 and 1600cc. form, with 5 speed manual gearboxes on each or the 3 speed automatic on the 1.5 litre version. All these engines were identical to those used in the Delta range and, not surprisingly, delivered very similar performances. The wheelbase of the two models was identical but the overall length of the Prisma went up to 4180mm from the 3885mm of the Delta. Weight also increased, though not to any great extent and even the heaviest, the 1600, was some 25kg lighter than the HF Delta.

Apart from external changes, the major redesign that took place was of the interior. At last, taller passengers had a little more headroom and more room for their legs, though at the expense of space from the driver. Middle-aged men with expanding midriffs were better off in the Delta, which offered them 560mm for their girth against only 521 in the Prisma. They had a better view of the instruments

A four wheel drive Prisma on an Alpine photocall.
Although Lancia total traction is now firmly
associated with the Delta, the Prisma was actually
the first production 4x4 to be put into production
by the company.

in the new car, however, for the dashboard and steering wheel were redesigned to be more visible and less obstructive then in the Delta. Occupants of all shapes and sizes were generally more comfortable in the new Prisma seats, which, although not completely overcoming the firm suspension, offered good lateral support. The rear seats were also capable of being folded down to allow increased luggage capacity, a facility only otherwise available in a Saab.

On the road the car was innocently described by *Quattroruote* as a woman of brilliance. Feminism has a tenuous hold in Italy. What the tester meant, apparently, was that the car was elegant, well-appointed and alert. In most respects it performed like the Delta. Acceleration was good, top speed, at between 160 and 178kph for the three capacities, was more than adequate and the range of options, from air conditioning to trip computer all that should be expected from a car of its class and aspiration. The only thing to have changed for the worse, depending of course on point of view and skill, was the Prisma's cornering. Like the Delta it was set up to understeer but unlike the shorter, two box car the Prisma, particularly with a laden boot, would go quickly into oversteer if pushed too far. The portly middle-aged might not have liked that. On the other hand, the portly middle-aged might once have been slim and speedy, in which case a Prisma with its tail out was just the thing.

4 S4

CLOSE TO THE western end of the Corso Francia, one of those great Torinese thoroughfares that are so unItalian in their directness, lies the Corso Marche. The old Abarth factory, now owned by Fiat, occupies most of it. Like the Corso itself, the factory is not large. In all it probably covers three blocks, but its significance to Fiat and Lancia is greater by far than its scale, for behind its well guarded gates the works rally cars are built.

Abarth came under Agnelli control in 1972, the year Fiat broke its self-imposed moratorium on works supported motor sport by entering two 124 Spyders in the British RAC Rally. Not since 1927, when Fiat won its last race, the Milan Grand Prix,

with Tranquillo Zerbi's remarkable 1.5 litre supercharged twin six engined Tipo 806, had the factory provided formal support for competition cars. Whether it was pure coincidence that Fiat returned to competition in the same year that they saved Carlo Abarth from bankruptcy is hard to say. At the least it was fortuitous, for Abarth and for Fiat.

Once the Group B rules governing international rallying had been breached by the Stratos in 1975, Lancia's engineers allowed their imaginations to blossom. The culmination of this inventive flowering was the wonderful, difficult and ultimately deadly S4 Delta.

The S4 was unveiled at the Abarth factory on Turin's Corso Marche on December 13th, 1984. Design work had begun early in 1983, under the direction of the great Aurelio Lampredi, but by the time the car appeared control of the project had passed to Claudio Lombardi.

By the adoption of both super and turbo charging the S4 offered a genuinely radical solution to the problems of forced induction in rally cars. By going even further and adopting a most sophisticated form of four wheel drive set in a state of the art chassis, Lancia's engineers excelled themselves and devastated the rallying competiton.

Carlo Abarth arrived in Turin from his native Austria in 1947 to work on Piero Dusio's ambitious Grand Prix Cisitalia. He was part of an especially talented design team consisting of Ferry Porsche, Eberan van Eberhurst and Julius Rabe. The Grand Prix antecedents of the group lay in the pre-war Auto Union and it is conceivable that the proposals they brought to Cisitalia contained much of the thinking that would, under other circumstances, have gone into the German car. What they planned was stunning. Their 306 Cisitalia would have a twin overhead camshaft, 1.5 litre flat twelve engine, supercharged and rear-mounted, capable of developing around 300bhp. What was more, this power was put onto the road through a sophisticated, selectable four wheel drive transmission which was so far ahead of its time and of Dusio's purse that only one 360 was built, and that broke the company. But before then, in 1949, Abarth, with some foresight, sought out premises in Turin, where he set up shop on his own in April of that year.

From then until the early 1970's he produced a fascinating and generally successful string of Fiat

S4 cockpit. For all its sophistication – or perhaps because of it – the S4 was a most difficult car to drive and Fiorio, the team manager, wondered occasionally whether anyone had ever been able to take it to the limit.

based sports cars. Best known were those derived from the Fiat 600 and, in particular, the beautiful, tiny ' double bubble' Zagato 750 and 850 coupes. Such a close relationship with Fiat led, however, to inevitable absorption when the money ran out. The Abarth company had a good twenty years of independence but towards the end, at which time it was closely involved with Siata, the Spanish dependency of Fiat, it became increasingly difficult to stand alone. So in went Abarth, out went Carlo, and his company with its Scorpion symbol became the competition arm of the Agnelli empire, under the sole direction of Aurelio Lampredi.

At the time of the Fiat Abarth merger Lancia, only two years into their own Fiat novitiate, still ran their competition cars from the old Squadra Corse headquarters in the Borgo San Paolo, just around the block from the factory in the Via Vincenzo Lancia. Under Gianni Lancia's directions, the racing B20's, the 'D' series sports and D50 Grand Prix cars had all emerged from these workshops and later, in the 1960's, Cesare Fiorio revived the running elephant motif with the HF Squadra Corse Flavias, Flaminias and Fulvias. Eventually, however, with Fiat in the saddle, all this changed. In 1977 Squadra Corse Lancia was wound up and the cars taken over by a new, corporate team, Squadra Corse Unificata, directed by Fiorio.

With this, Lancia moved to the Corso Marche workshops where they bided their time until, in January 1983, planning began for their newest, most advanced rally car, the 038 Delta S4. Lancia needed it. Since 1977 they had been out of the World Rally Championship as a result of Fiat policy, but now, at last, as a result of external forces, things were changing and in 1982 Lancia built a wholly new car, the 037, with which to go rallying in the new Group B category of the latest FISA rules. It was a great relief to old company hands in the competition department. Even though the 037 was a stopgap machine, one distantly derived from the Monte Carlo road and silhouette cars, it did at least have the right pedigree and was novel enough to live up to Lancia's reputation. Supercharged, not a turbo; two wheel drive at the back, not four; Abarth four in line motor, not six and not a V, the 037 Lancia Rally Abarth was a one-off, an original.

Its purpose was to meet a need and buy time. The 1980's would see great changes in rallying, changes already announced by the FIA which Fiat could not ignore. From 1982 an entirely new version of the 'Appendix J', the competition vehicle rule book, would come into force and Fiat, like its competitors, could not afford to be caught out; as a consequence, Lancia were brought back into play, since their image was more suited to what was to come.

The old Appendix J, with its Group 1 to Group 5 categories, had been in operation for years. By and large it worked well, particularly for production cars, but from the early 1970's, with the emergence of cars like the Renault Alpine and Lancia's Stratos, it was obvious that manufacturers had found ways of bending the rules. What they had managed to do was find a loophole in the homologation regulations which allowed them to do exactly what the rules were designed to prevent, namely buying victory with costly, high-performance specialist competition cars at the expense of more open sport between the drivers of mass-produced machines.

Homologation is a process of verification. It

To homologate the S4 rally car, Lancia had to build a street version for sale to the general public. 200 cars had to have been built and be available for inspection by FISA officials before the competition version could contest the Championship.

Undressed, the S4 Stradale shows all of the distinguishing characteristics of the full house S4. Although built of less expensive materials than the racer and fitted with a de-tuned engine, this remarkable road going 4x4 must be one of the rarest and most distinctive cars in the world.

establishes compatibility among different cars by demanding certain requirements which all must fulfil in order to compete in particular categories. The starting point for these requirements was the mass-produced car. By this was meant a minimum production of 5000 vehicles. Under Appendix J these could be either saloons, in Groups 1 and 2 or GT cars in Groups 3 and 4, with Group 5 reserved for prototypes. In these categories, Groups 2 and 4 were available to more highly tuned version of cars in Groups 1 and 3, which only needed to be produced in minimum batches of 400. When the rules were originally framed the reduced production quantities for the tuned cars were expected to apply to special components only. As time passed, however, the number of such components in a car multiplied until it seemed quite sensible to build complete Group 4 cars (in particular) from scratch. Which is what Lancia did with the Stratos.

But from 1982 the homologation rules were to change. Out with numerical groups and in with letters. The new groups A, B and N catered for minimum production of 5000, 200 and 5000 respectively. Groups A and B imposed identical tuning regulations, while Group N required less performance than Group A. Thus, in effect, Appendix J became a set of manufacturing regulations, providing identical tuning controls to both volume and limited production cars. Under such circumstances Fiat obviously needed to hand the ball back to Lancia, for it was plain to everyone that Group B was where the action would be found.

The decision to build the 037 Rally Abarth was taken in 1980. Lampredi designed the supercharged engine and responsibility for the rest of the car lay with two other engineers, Limone and Messori, colleagues of Gianni Tonti, the great Lancia engineer responsible for so much of the company's success since the days of the Fulvia. It was homologated on April 1st, 1982 and in 1983 won the World Rally Championship, demonstrating, as it did so, that two good Lancia wheels were more than a match for four from Audi.

Yet it was not a trick that could be easily repeated. Without more power and more traction the Italian cars would be unable to cope with the Quattro in future competitions. Nor could they contain the new challenge emerging from Peugeot's 205 Turbo, with its 4WD, 350bhp and 340kph. The need for the S4 was pressing.

Within months of receiving approval for the project, S4 development was well in hand. Very few demands were made of Lampredi's team, other than that the car should relate to the production

Delta in some way. On their blank sheets of paper the designers therefore dutifully wrote the name 'Delta', penciled in a body with some distant resemblance to the street car and then got on with producing something remarkable.

Everyone in the small team knew the extent of their difficulties. Unlike their counterparts at Weissach, where Audi employed designers and technicians in great numbers and provided them with the most sophisticated laboratory facilities, Fiat required the team to be kept comparatively small. Not that they were denied resources. The parent company put up the cash and provided generous support. The problem was that the research facilities were scattered across Turin: what Lampredi and his team lacked was that concentration of expertise and hardware available to such as Audi and Porsche, where competition development went hand in hand with that of road cars.

The difference in approach was summarised in a *Quattroruote* interview with Audi's Ferdinand Piech and Lancia's Cesare Fiorio. Six identical questions were put to each concerning four wheel drive rally cars. One question asked whether it would be sensible for teams to field two types of car, one with two wheel drive for asphalt and a 4X4 for loose surfaces. Fiorio thought this reasonable, going so far as to suggest that Lancia might at some time do just this. Piech, on the other hand, said 'It's possible, but absolutely outside our way of seeing things. We want to make the best cars and we race to show they are the best; winning is not the most important thing. For us what is important is to be best and consequently the cars have to be best under all conditions.' Two fundamentally different philosophies were at work here. Fiorio and Lancia built limited numbers of exotic rally cars that bore no relation to their commercial production: Piech and Audi rallied with specially prepared road cars. The development implications were as obvious as the national traits. Everyone in Audi looked to the same goals; at Fiat everyone carried their own torch. Yet the results were similar, though as far as innovation, technical flair and rapid development were concerned, the Lancia team were as good as any. Unfortunately in the 4X4 stakes they started from well behind.

The shape that emerged in the first few months was utterly radical and when the S4 was revealed publicly for the first time on December 13th 1984, it caused some surprise, the more so because Lancia's security had been almost totally leak proof. By the time of the launch, nearly two years after design work began, responsibility for the car had passed to

Claudio Lombardi, Abarth's recently appointed technical director. The initial concept, devised by Lampredi and Limone, remained intact. Sadly, however, after the svelte elegance of the 037 and its memorable predecessor, the Stratos, the 038 was an ugly duckling. It was better looking than the 131 but only just. In fact it was something of a lump, what the French would call *'une jolie laide'*, suggesting it was so ugly it was beautiful. But whatever surprise the packaging caused was nothing compared to the contents: as so often in the past, Lancia had done it again.

The white, Martini-striped car presented to the press in the spacious 'works' preparation area at the Corso Marche factory was the most powerful Group B contender yet produced. The intense gestation it had undergone resulted in genuinely radical solutions to the problems of forced induction and chassis construction, while its four wheel drive system, similar in many ways to that adopted by Ford for their RS2000, was as near to the optimum as possible. Together these innovations resulted in a formidable Group B World Championship car, producing more than 400 bhp at 8000 rpm in a chassis weighing 890kg and putting its power down through all four wheels in what would hopefully be a wholly controllable fashion. It was a thoroughly modern monster.

But what made it special? Certainly none of the systems on their own were in any way revolutionary. Supercharging, turbocharging, space frame construction, kevlar panels and four wheel drive were all common, if not commonplace. Rather, what made the S4 unique was what had made other Lancias at other times unique: the combination of all these tried technologies in one, new, refreshing vehicle. This had been old Vincenzo Lancia's strength and this was still the inspiration that underlay the company in 1984.

To begin with the engine. By the time the S4 project got underway, Abarth, Fiat and Lancia knew a lot about twin cam, in-line, four valve fours. Although not characteristic of Lancia Engineering, the Endurance Racing team had done a lot with this traditional Fiat motor in the Beta Monte Carlo Turbo. Under the direction of Gianni Tonti, the team's engineers extracted 420bhp at 8800rpm and 1.6 atmospheres of boost from a 1.4 litre version: by 1981 this figure had risen to 490bhp at 8000rpm from 1.7 litres and twin turbos, all of which work was of undoubted interest to the S4 design team.

The latest Lancia version of Fiat's old retainer, now wearing Abarth cam covers, also displaced 1.7 litres or, more precisely 1759cc. It was an all alloy, undersquare short stroke unit whose dimensions of 88.5 x 71.5mm gave a bore/stroke ratio of 0.81. Set fore and aft and 20 degrees left of vertical, the engine was carried in a sub frame assembly which allowed for easy removal, the more so once the whole rear end of the body was swung up and out of the way.

Flat crowned pistons on steel rods ran on a five bearing crank in integral, Cerametal-hardened liners. The compression ratio was 7:1. Dry sump lubrication was by twin scavenge and single delivery pumps.

But the most interesting aspect of the engine from the point of view of the various engineers, rallyists, journalists and rivals who saw it first on that December day, was its dual system of forced induction. After much experiment with supercharging and turbos and much argument about the merits and drawbacks of each, Lancia's engineers took the decision of Solomon and had both. Their thinking was sound, if expensive. They knew that superchargers, being crankshaft driven, use engine power and above a certain output the law of diminishing returns sets in. This normally occurs around 6/7000 supercharger rpm, beyond which speed more power is consumed than is generated. However, at low engine rpm more power is generated than is absorbed. What is more, this power is continuously available. Turbochargers, on the other hand, only generate power when there is sufficient exhaust gas flow to spin the turbine rapidly, which means that power delivery fluctuates. However, at high rpm and maximum torque, a considerable increase in power becomes available. What could be more sensible, therefore, than to provide both systems as complementary in one engine. Lampredi, Lombardi, Limone and Carlo Pangallo all agreed and the S4 engine was therefore built with an Abarth supercharger and a KKK turbo. The supercharger was geared up to 1.16:1 and fitted with an air bypass which reduced pressure as rpm rose. With the rise in engine speed and the drop in supercharger boost, the turbo cut in and power continued to rise, reaching a maximum at 35 psi turbo boost.

If this potent combination of technologies put Lancia well ahead of their rivals, the package containing it put them in a different league. Recognising that power was one thing but weight was another, the design team produced a chassis weighing less than 100kg as a stripped frame. It was built of chrome molybdenum steel tube and constructed in such a way as to give great torsional rigidity,

Competition engine (above) and street cockpit (below). A potential power output of over 500bhp was anticipated but the most pressing problem facing the engineers was how to put it onto the road. The Stradale presented no such difficulties from its 250bhp at 6750rpm.

deflecting only one degree under a load of 1500kgm. This was a better figure than that achieved for the Stratos, which twisted its degree under a mere 1300kgm. Both figures, of course, came near those of contemporary Formula One cars: they also put into perspective the brilliance of Lancia's funny old Aprilia, another stiffnecked creation which moved only 0°10′ under a load of 125kgm!

In the S4, stiffness was a product of its bonded kevlar roof and other vacuum-formed 5mm honeycomb panels of kevlar, Nomex and carbonfibre, in combination with the lightweight chassis. Such extensive use of advanced materials enabled the designers to cope with the additional weight penalty imposed by the four wheel drive transmission yet still bring the car close to the minimum weight of 890kgs allowed in its class.

The move to four wheel drive was inevitable, given the high proportion of loose surfaces encountered in most World Championship events. Even

The S4 Stradale press launch occurred in the Autumn of 1985. A group of journalists were taken to the island of Elba to try the car in undemanding circumstances. All enjoyed it, but those who thought to draw conclusions about the rally version from their brief spin on the road were sadly misled.

though Fiorio insisted that 4X4 systems were not, in themselves, the solution to all the problems of rallying, he recognised their superiority on gravel. However, he remained to be convinced that on asphalt four driven wheels were better than two, particularly since the S4, under test, proved as reluctant to change direction as the Stratos had proved too willing. Nevertheless, changes in direction had to come and, short of supporting entirely different designs of car for different rally conditions – an expensive operation even for Lancia – four wheel drive was now necessary.

The system chosen was similar to that used by Ford for their RS2000, but better thought out. Ford, for reasons best known to themselves, put the weight of their transmission at the front of the car. This necessitated a double, four piece propeller shaft with no less than six universal joints and did little to counteract the innate understeer of 4X4 drive systems with too much frontal mass. Lancia, by contrast, sought to achieve a low polar moment, as in the old D50 GP car and the later Stratos. This meant mass in the middle. The five speed Hewland/Lancia gearbox was therefore bolted to the front of the engine with the centre differential integral with it and located in the middle of the car. In

Unlike the earlier and highly successful Audi Quattro, Lancia's S4 was a low polar moment car, like their old and capricious D50 GP car of the mid 1950's. Low polar moment makes for rapid changes in direction, something very necessary in a rally car. Unfortunately, in early tests some changes were quite unpredictable.

the prototype this centre differential was mechanical, with torque split being varied by changing gear clusters. This was a temporary arrangement until a Ferguson type viscous differential was ready. The viscous coupling, which consisted of drilled, alternate discs connected to opposite output shafts and running in a silicon based fluid, allowed the driver to precisely control the torque split between front and rear axles. It was also possible to lock it to give either a 50/50 split or total rear wheel drive. The benefits of such choice were obvious in a World Championship with events ranging from the snow and ice of Sweden, through the unpredictable mixture of asphalt and ice of the Monte Carlo to the dusty gravel of the Acropolis and the mud of Kenya.

S4 suspension followed 037 design. It was fully adjustable and rose jointed with long travel double wishbones front and rear. Single Bilstein spring/shock absorbers were fitted at the front with double dampers, similar to the 037, at the back. Large sixteen inch wheels, betraying a certain circuit racing ancestry, were fitted with 8J 230/45-16 Pirelli P7's at the front and 12h290/660-16 P7's at the rear. Power assisted steering was fitted, with the promise

of an air assisted system, without pumps and oil, to follow later.

Testing the S4, getting it right, took a long time. Giorgio Pianta had responsibility for this. Pianta had been with Lancia for years. He was an experienced driver from Flavia and Fulvia days and an engineer and tester of great skill who worked on the Stratos, the Monte Carlo Turbo, the LC cars and the 037. When Fiat pushed Lancia into Squadra Unificata, Pianta was appointed Head Tester and it was in this capacity that he took on the S4, assisted by another lifelong member of Squadra Lancia HF, chief mechanic Luigino Podda.

The reasons why S4 development took so long were both complex and banal. The roll-out took place at Christmas 1984, but it was to be another 12 months before the first World Championship appearance occurred. As had happened with previous cars, production was delayed as parts failed to materialise and deadlines came and went. The parts problem was perhaps the most serious. When development began, immediately after the December launch, there were only two prototypes available. Because of the highly innovative nature of the car, many components were specially made and expensive. When they broke they were not always immediately replaceable; such failure also required analysis, for the S4 was not only seen by Fiat as a race car but as a test bed for other, more commercially relevant projects. Development was consequently slow. Lombardi and his colleague, engineer Pier Paolo Messori, were learning as they went along, without any substantial previous experience of four wheel drive systems, or of compound forced induction to fall back on.

The difficulties facing them were numerous. For Lombardi, developing an engine capable of ultimately producing 500bhp was only half the matter: when that power was put on to the road through all four wheels, the real development questions emerged. In rallying the balance of the car on unpredictable surfaces is an essential part of success. With two wheel drive systems, whether front or rear, the factors governing balance and control were well known. With four wheel systems this was not the case, as Pianta discovered when he first took the car out for serious work.

Consequently, during the first six months of testing the real issues facing the team concerned power split, the development of effective slip limitation in each of the three differentials and, most difficult of all, setting the car up in such a way as to allow the driver to select two wheel drive when appropriate and still retain control. This was not easy. Initially the car demonstrated serious power understeer. Experienced drivers could control it through left foot braking but this was not ideal. The S4's geometry was also set up to cope with four driven wheels; when drive was shifted to the rear alone, further problems arose. Then there was the ironic situation of a low polar moment car that was reluctant to change direction easily – oh, there were so many, many problems.

Yet, inevitably, as 1985 progressed, they were solved. In April Pianta, with team members Alen and Kivimaki, was in Sardinia, testing the car on the Costa Smeralda. With only four months to go (including the dead period of the Italian August) before the S4's planned entry in the World Championship in Finland's Thousand Lakes Rally, his task was immense. With the Ferguson viscous coupling not yet arrived from England, testing was still being done using a mechanical centre differential. This held up development. The motor and gearbox were fine, according to Alen, but the handling left much to be desired, particularly downhill when the machine was sometimes uncontrollable. It could also be unpredictable in a straight line.

But entry into the Finnish rally did not only depend upon getting the car right. Another, even less predictable matter, that of homologation, beset Fiorio and his colleagues. The deadline for this, if the Thousand Lakes was to be open to the S4, was August 1st, by which time 200 versions of the detuned roadgoing S4 had to have been built and available for sale. By June, when Pianta and Alen returned to the Costa Smeralda for further tests, this time with a redesigned, larger supercharger and not only a Ferguson centre diff but with viscous systems front and rear as well, only 50 S4 Stradale's were complete and the prospect of Finland faded, despite Lancia's wildly confident gesture in booking an homologation inspection for July 20th.

Failure to meet homologation deadlines was not new to Lancia. The Stratos had many false dawns before finally becoming legal, and even then there had been doubts about the actual number of cars built and ready for sale. The S4 merely followed precedent in this matter and the Thousand Lakes came and went without the new Lancia. The pattern was repeated in September, when Fiorio tried again and failed to gain homologation in time for San Remo. After that, all that was left of the 1985 World Rally Championship was the RAC. The British rally was never popular with Fiorio and had circumstances been different he would not have dreamt of launching his new car in such an unpred-

An early, pre homologation competition test of the S4's abilities occurred in Italy's Colline di Romagna Rally. An initial, but subsequently wrong impression of a fragile, fast machine was gained by outside observers.

ictable, winter event. He had little choice in the matter, however. The 200th road going S4 was not completed until November. Homologation was achieved on December 1st and if the S4 was to appear in the '85 World Championship, its debut had to be British.

Prior to the RAC the car ran in several lesser events outside the Championship. It appeared first in Sardinia, in the Costa Smeralda rally, then in France, in the Mille Pistes and in Italy in the Colline di Romagna rally. These outings obviously amounted to more than flag waving, providing the team with valuable experience of the car and enabling them to test its complexity in the unforgiving world of competition. They also allowed journalists to gain impressions and out of the various, inevitable breakdowns which occurred was formed a general view of a fragile car. Fiorio, ever the strategist, turned this to advantage, however, and in November, at a press day held during pre-RAC testing in Scotland, allowed journalists to speculate on whether the car was quite the Audi/Peugeot eater they expected.

LEFT **Claudio Lombardi, the engineer responsible for the devastating success of the Delta 4x4 and Integrale in the Group A World Championship, took over control of the S4 project just before the car's public unveiling. His engineering skills married perfectly with Cesare Fiorio's unmatched talent for rally management.**

BELOW **'Vista in trasparenza' of the S4; supercharging, turbocharging, four wheel drive, and despite the technical complexity, it would soon prove its durability and driveability.**

A few weeks earlier, in the warmth of Elba, many of the same journalists had briefly sampled the road going version of the S4 at the pre-homologation launch. Detuned to 250bhp at 6750rpm, the street legal limited edition shared all the eccentric character of its Group B sister. The only significant changes lay in the gearbox (with syncromesh rather than dog engagement), the transmission, the substitution of steel for titanium wherever possible, the use of smaller super and turbo charges and thinner brake discs. The interior was fully trimmed of course and the impression given to most of the scribes was of a comfortable, fascinating but wholly unterrifying machine. All of which contrived to suggest to the opposition that perhaps Lancia had got it wrong with the S4.

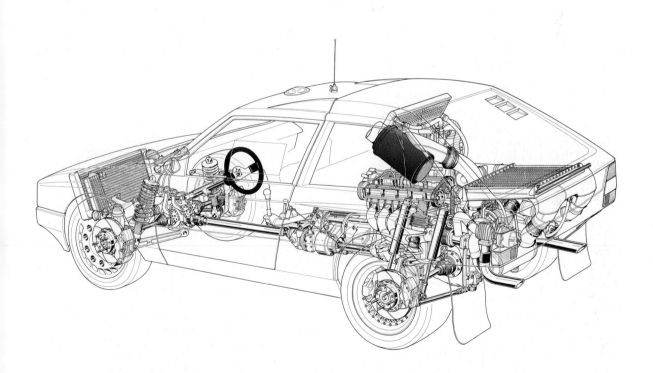

5   Death in Sardinia

THE 1985 RAC RALLY started at 8 a.m. on November 24th from Wollaston Hall, near Nottingham. There were 155 starters, two of which were S4's. When it finished on November 28th only 62 were left but the S4's, driven by Henri Toivonen and Markku Alen were 1st and 2nd. Not a bad debut.

Until well into the rally it was hard to know whether Lancia were taking it seriously or not. They went into the event in third place in the World Championship, having contested only four of the possible ten rallies prior to the RAC. They were therefore in no position to pull off a last minute victory as they had done 11 years earlier with the belatedly homologated Stratos. There was something less than committed about their organisation. They did not always have enough spares in the right place; Toivonen had not driven the car on gravel before the event; some of the crew were booked on a flight back to Turin that was to leave before the final stages were complete; it all seemed uncharacteristically careless, for Lancia were nothing if not one of the most professional outfits in rallying. There were other signs too, stemming perhaps from Fiorio's dislike of the event. Even before it began he threatened to pull the cars out when the scrutineers objected to the list of sponsors on the doors of the S4's, a list which contravened the regulations forbidding any promotion on the doors other than Lombard, the rally sponsors. Fortunately, such was the attraction of the cars, the organisers relented but when the rally was over and with an unexpected victory in his pocket, Fiorio returned to the attack.

What bothered him, and many other team bosses and drivers, was the secret nature of the RAC. Traditionally it was the one rally in the World calendar that did not allow practice and the consequent production of pace notes. Drivers like Walter Rohrl hated the event and after the '85 rally Jean Todt, Peugeot team manager, spoke for most manufacturers in expressing his fears for the safety of drivers and spectators now that Group B cars had become so powerful. Fiorio agreed with him and urged that the RAC be brought into line with other World Championship events.

Lack of practice did not, however, deter either Toivonen or Alen from extracting the most from their S4's. Far from being sheep in wolve's clothing, the cars quickly proved to be devastatingly fast, so much so that Tony Pond, who finished third in the new MG R64, was reported as saying, 'If I drive as fast as the Lancias, I shall have an accident. They keep getting back on – if I did it I'd stay off.' What this remark also highlighted was the sheer strength of the S4, which was not the fragile, over complicated machine many had imagined. When it rolled it usually stayed in one piece.

The first stages of the rally were short sprints, thought of by of the many drivers as Mickey Mouse

ABOVE RIGHT **The S4's first World Championship event was the Lombard RAC Rally. This was the last event of the 1985 calender and important for Lancia prestige. Yet the cars may well not have started. Fiorio threatened to withdraw them when the organisers objected to some of their adverts.**

RIGHT **For comparison, the front end of the Integrale, a foretaste of what was to come just a couple of years later: stretched wheel arches and more air for the uprated 2 litre engine; (see Ch 8.)**

sections. Neither Alen nor Toivonen shared this view. The sheer straight line speed and the stability of the new cars was instantly established by Alen, who won five of the first seven short stages before the Forest of Dean. Toivonen, driving with Welshman Neil Wilson as navigator, was slower, though he took the 3 mile Trentham stage by a clear 3 seconds from Hannu Mikkola's Quattro.

Having established their credentials, the two Lancia drivers settled down to prove their S4's on the increasingly tough terrains that followed. This did not turn out to be easy. As if to confirm the sceptical view of the cars as quick but of uncertain temperament, the tough South Wales stages took the shine off Lancia's promising start. Alen's engine began to misfire and stall and by the time Swansea was reached he had slipped to third place

ABOVE **By the time the S4 arrived on the scene, the sheer speed of Group B cars was already beginning to cause concern among some drivers and managers. The new Lancia, with its staggering performance, produced even more anxiety, though few of the doubters voiced their concerns with any force.**

ABOVE RIGHT **Toivonen in the '85 RAC. No respecter of cars, Henri rearranged the S4 bodywork on several occasions as well as suffering various mechanical problems on his way to a first victory for the previously untried car.**

RIGHT **The S4 worked wonderfully under all conditions – gravel, dust, mud, snow, ice and tarmac.**

with Toivonen sixth. But the journey north through the Welsh forests allowed them to recover. Despite their share of mechanical and human mishaps they kept going, unlike Mikkola and Salonen, the leaders in the Quattro and Peugeot 205 respectively. Salonen retired at Dyfi and Mikkola went out on the next stage, Cwmcelli, with ignition failure. Immediately after this Malcolm Wilson blew up his R64 engine and the Lancias were back in the lead.

Fuel supply problems dogged both cars as the day continued. On Dyfnant 2, the last Welsh stage, Toivonen's car lost time when it ran out of fuel (though remarkable good luck provided them with more, supplied by a bystander with a can!) and only

ABOVE **Henri Toivonen, a charismatic driver whose father had driven for Lancia in the days of the Fulvia. The S4, with its temperament and power was well suited to the young Finn's talent.**

BELOW **Mikki Biasion talks tactics with team boss Cesare Fiorio. Fiorio's profound knowledge of rallying often gave his drivers the edge when competition was close.**

Tragedy at Sintra, the first stage of the 1986 Portuguese Rally led to a drivers strike. Lack of crowd control made the event unsafe in the minds of many drivers. As a result all of the major teams, including Lancia, withdrew from the rally. Walter Rohrl, seen here with other drivers, was unfairly criticised by the Portuguese authorities, who allowed the rally to continue despite the protest. For many spectators, the Portuguese event was a sort of mechanised bullfight.

after some further stages of high fuel consumption did Giorgio Pianta and his crew discover the cause. In another surprisingly careless piece of preparation the cars had been fitted with the wrong type of petrol tanks, which led to pick up failure at the pumps when the level was low. The only cure was to keep the tanks full, which Toivonen particularly resented, preferring for obvious reasons to run with minimum fuel loads.

The halfway point at Nottingham saw Lancia still in the lead. In the available service time Alen's

LEFT **Markku Alen had considerable experience of the Tour de Corse. In the 1986 event he drove one of the latest, lighter S4's. His team mate Henri Toivonen had another new car and the third member of the Lancia team, Mikki Biasion, drove his Portuguese car.**

BELOW LEFT **For Toivonen, the Corsican event was a new experience. More a tortuous, high speed road race than a rally, the Tour demanded extensive practice. Henri and his navigator, Sergio Cresto, invested much in preparation but in the end the event killed them. The Group B cars exacted too great a price.**

BELOW **Mikael Ericsson, Toivonen's replacement, gets the S4 airborne in Greece.**

car had its gearbox and rear differential changed and later, at Carlisle, Toivonen's S4 was similarly overhauled. The durability of the transmission was still a source of concern for the team, even though, for the RAC, the cars were running on old style mechanical differentials front and rear and a front/rear torque split of 30/70. Since the transmission had given trouble in the Algarve, precautions seemed sensible in Britain.

Up in the literally frozen north of the Keilder stages, Alen continued to hold his lead through a mixture of bad and good luck. Toivonen's drive was also proving eventful, the Finn moving back into second place ahead of Tony Pond only after a monumental roll which flung navigator Wilson's glasses into the bowels of the car but otherwise caused little damage. Alen's good luck came second time round on Keilder, when he ran out of road, only to be pulled out by Juha Kankkunen and his Celica, an act of generosity that earned the rescuer a reprimand from his boss.

So the rally continued, with Alen, Toivonen and Pond fighting for control. Eventually, however, Toivonen, despite further transmission and supercharger problems, took the lead from Alen, whose hold over Pond and the Metro was confirmed when the British driver chose the wrong tyres for the icy 59th stage at Wythorp. And that was how it finished: Toivonen first, Alen second and Pond third

Sergio Cresto, Henri Toivonen's Italian American co-driver was highly respected despite a comparative lack of World Championship experience. In a high speed event like the Tour de Corse, the navigator was, as ever, an essential part of the team. Death at an early age was unexpected.

The cause of Toivenen's fatal accident in Corsica was never satisfactorily established. All that could be said afterwards was that rallying lost two of its bright stars. That Group B also died was ultimately of no importance.

BELOW Daniel Cerrato in a Totip sponsored S4 during the Italian round of the '86 World Championship at San Remo.

ABOVE **Local driver Jorge Recalde joined Alen and Biasion for the Argentine Rally which immediately preceded San Remo. The South American event was won by Biasion. Lancia were glad of the points.**

BELOW **Fiorio, seen here with Lombardi at a press conference, joined Lancia in the early 1960's. His enthusiasm and dedication led to the formation of HF Squadra Corse in 1965. The successes of the following years were due in large part to him.**

– an unexpected triumph all round for new, untried cars from Lancia and Austin. The next task for the Italians was to establish a new dominance and see the R64, the Quattro and the 205 sink into oblivion.

The brief Christmas pause between one year's Championship and the next allowed Lancia to complete its preparations for the Monte, the first event of '86. The front line team for the season comprised Alen/Kivimaki, Toivonen and Sergio Cresto, a new Italian American member of the squad and Biasion/Siviero. All were equipped with S4's, though the old 037 was kept in service for the Safari, in particular.

The 1986 Championship was preceded by the usual rash of rule changed introduced by FISA, the Paris based governing body. Grappling with the

By drawing together all of their initial 4×4 research with the experience gained in rallying the S4, Lancia were able to put the most effective total traction system yet devised straight into their production 4×4's and the Group A cars.

regulations was becoming as demanding as running their cars for many team managers and rally organisers. Of particular significance was the requirement that all teams be registered with FISA in order to be eligible for World Championship points. Only registered drivers could be nominated and nominations had to be made before entries closed. This led to confusion as the season passed, though not for Lancia, who, at Monte Carlo, had enough mechanical alarms and excursions to keep them busy without getting caught up in bureaucracy.

Their Round One troubles began early, with Alen suffering first. On the concentration run to Aix les Bains from his starting point at Sestriere his engine misfired continually. Even before setting off, during the final evening's preparations, he had had an oil pump belt break. The next day, on the Bergamo autostrada, a camshaft went. This was rapidly replaced but the engine was still down on power. All in all, Lancia's senior driver felt himself lucky to get into the rally at all.

Toivonen and Biasion had fewer initial difficul-

ties and on the first special stage the young Italian driver went into the lead. This state of affairs did not last, and by the time the rally left Aix, Toivonen was ahead with Alen second, despite his still misfiring engine, and Biasion down to third. Things could not be better from Lancia's point of view. Everything continued to go well until Stage 12 at Burzet. Despite such minor troubles as Toivonen setting his brakes alight and Alen breaking the oil pump belt yet again, the Lancias remained in front. Rohrl, who had been coming back strongly in the Quattro, suffered some loss of time after being forced to fit a studded spare when conditions were dry and as a result Toivonen's lead steadily lengthened. Then came disaster. Coming out of Burzet the S4 was hit head-on by a private car. It was severely damaged and Henri's rally seemed over. With a wheel knocked off, the oil cooler ruptured and the front body shattered, it looked impossible to repair. Yet repaired it was. Although seriously bent, with the wheel base on one side shorter than the other, the car was miraculously made driveable again. Equally miraculous was Toivonen's willing-

ness not just to drive it, but to drive it fast. In fact, he went so well that he won the rally. Other competitors nicknamed the car the banana and suggested that if it could be made to win in such a condition Lancia ought to bend all the rest. Alen probably agreed. He retired on Stage 17 with a broken camshaft. Miki Biasion also went out after an accident on stage 26.

Three weeks later Toivonen and Alen found themselves in Scandinavia for the 36th Swedish Rally. This had never been a good event for Lancia but now, with a total traction car, the Italians hoped for a good result. Their optimism was reinforced by the organiser's decision to allow extra tyre studs to be fitted. For several seasons the question of studded tyres and their supposed road damaging capacity had been a vexed one. In

Delta HF 4WD engine, photographed at the launch at San Remo in 1986. This new engine was based on the well proven 2 litre dohc unit used in the Thema and characterised by its vibration damping counter balance shafts.

Development of the HF4WD had been continuous since the 4×4 prototype appeared in 1982. First news of the new car came in 1985 but it did not appear until a year later. As soon as it was available, amateur rally drivers took it straight into Italian Group N events.

Argentina 1986. Biasion on his way to winning the event from Alen, who was required to hold back as a result of team orders. Total traction made light work of river beds.

general the number permitted had been officially reduced to 12 per 10cm of tread circumference and length was also restricted. But with 1670km of mostly ice- and snow-covered stages before them, the decision to increase the permitted number was obviously welcome to all of the drivers.

Timo Salonen, the World Champion whom Toivonen had beaten into second place at Monaco, particularly welcomed the change. He had been a little put out to lose to the driver of a wreck, albeit a fast one, and set out to settle the score in Sweden. Over the first six stages between the start at Karlstad and Malung, the halfway point of the first Etape, his 205 Peugeot was unbeatable. Toivonen, driving well and now expressing himself to be fully happy with the Delta, had to be content with second place. Alen was less fortunate. Once again his engine lacked power and he struggled to stay in contact with the leaders. The source of the trouble proved difficult to find but was eventually traced to the supercharger. After it was changed, Alen's per-formance picked up and he moved to third place.

Salonen had by now retired, his engine on the verge of seizure after losing oil. This put Toivonen comfortable in the lead, followed by Kankkunen in the second 205 Peugeot. Everything looked set for another Lancia victory, until, on stage 13, the Lancia dropped an exhaust valve and Toivonen was out of the event. At this point Kankkunen's lead over Alen was considerable. All he had to do to win was stay out of trouble, which he did, giving Peugeot 20 points and putting them joint equal with the Lancia at the head of the World Championship.

Up to this point the 1986 season had been normal. The Group 3 supercars were not yet thought dangerously overpowered and the competition was good and exciting. But all this changed with the Portuguese Rally – changed profoundly and bloodily with three dead and many injured spectators, shocked and angry drivers and FISA in a panic. It happened suddenly but not unexpectedly. For years the problem of undisciplined crowds had grown and been neglected in Portugal. For many Portuguese fans, rallying had become a participatory and, for the most foolhardy, a contact sport. Young men filled the roads. It was a sign of bravery to stand your ground in the face of an oncoming

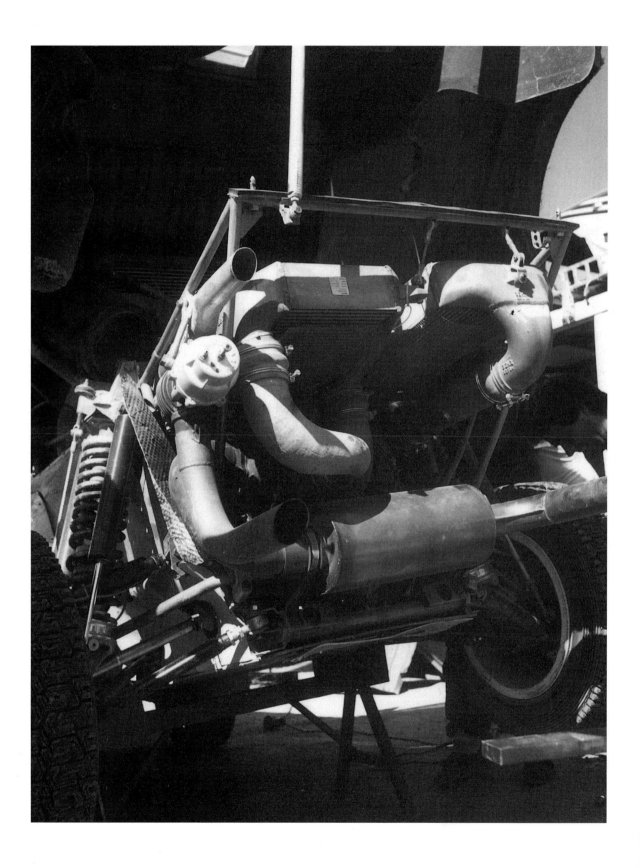

ABOVE **Alen, with helicopter support, beside the wine dark sea. Lancia never stinted on providing all necessary backup for their drivers, and in Greece such assistance was often necessary. Unfortunately it did not prevent the Finn from blowing up his engine.**

LEFT **Exposed rear end of S4 during service in the '86 Acropolis Rally. One of the design parameters given to the development team was ease of access to mechanical components.**

car, only leaping aside at the last minute and attempting to touch the car as it passed. Rallying was now mechanised bullfighting.

At Sintra, on the first stage just outside Lisbon, the price of this recklessness was finally paid. Joachim Santos came fast over the brow of a hill in his Ford RS200 to find spectators blocking the road. Although avoiding this first hazard, he was unnerved and spun off, killing and maiming many in the great press of people on and lining the road. Surprisingly – or perhaps not, given the organiser's seeming indifference to safety – the stage was not cancelled. Cars kept coming, though as soon as it was apparent that tragedy had occurred most drivers sought to pull out. Yet still the rally continued. The authorities appeared not to understand the drivers' reaction to the disaster and when, after a

further three desultory stages, all of the major teams voted to withdraw, there was outrage from Cesar Torres, Portugal's rally boss. He actually went so far as to suggest that Walter Rohrl had persuaded the other international team drivers to withdraw because he wanted the Portuguese Rally dropped from the Championship to make way for a German event! And a Lisbon newspaper, having railed against the drivers for denying the public its entertainment, pointed out that the odd death ought not be taken quite so seriously. There was a major breakdown in understanding.

The rally did continue but with without its stars. Lancia and the other manufacturers went home and the event was won by the Portuguese driver Joaquim Mortinho in a Renault. This unexpected result temporarily put him in second place with Henri Toivonen in the Drivers Championship.

Toivonen's next appearance for Lancia was in the Tour de Corse, held between May 1st and 3rd. He did not compete in the Safari, held a month earlier in Kenya, and was consequently full of energy and ambition to win. The S4 had also been rested, since Lancia chose to run their old 037 Ralleys for the last time in the African event they had struggled unsuccessfully for so long to win. Yet victory again eluded them, with Alen, despite a desperate final charge, only managing to finish third.

The points accrued in Kenya were enough,

Two wheel drive in Greece as Alen lifts the S4 off and back on to the road.

however, to put Lancia at the top of the table ahead of Peugeot by four points. This provided even greater incentives for the team to do well in Corsica. Three S4s were entered, driven by Alen, Biasion and Toivonen. Two of them, those of Alen and Toivonen, were new marginally lighter cars; Biasion drove his Portuguese Delta.

Toivonen, who was new to Corsica, put in extensive practice but each member of the team approached the event with care, ever mindful that in the previous year's event their promising team mate, Attilo Bettega, had been killed when his car crashed. Yet, however portentous, the tragedy was last year's tragedy; this year was another competition and points were not earned by caution. Nevertheless, it was not surprising that there was anxiety in the air. Many drivers were beginning to have doubts about the direction rally evolution was taking them. The cars were becoming as powerful as Formula One machines but were driven on public roads, not in the artificial environment of the closed circuit. They therefore sent a joint letter to

the organisers asking that some stages be shortened and others changed. It had no effect, which was something many were soon to regret, particularly in the Lancia camp for the day after the letter the Tour de Corse killed two more of the Turin team, Henri Toivonen and Sergio Cresto, who died when their S4 left the road at high speed and exploded on hitting the trees below. Such was the force of the impact the car was utterly destroyed. It was the end of Supercars in rallies. With the crash Group B died and, in the eyes of many, rallying took a step back towards sanity.

Immediately after the disaster, even before the Tour de Corse had finished and left the island, FISA's president, Jean-Marie Balestre, announced belated but drastic rule changes. All Group B evolution was to cease, certain body materials would be banned, special stages were to have a maximum length and duration, fire extinguishers would be mandatory (amazingly, they were not pre-Corsica), the proposed Group 5, intended to contain the otherwise unbridled evolutions of Group B, was cancelled and in future, most importantly, the World Rally Championship was to be exclusively for Group 'A' cars.

By the middle of the 1986 season Alen lay second to Kankkunen in the Drivers Championship. Lancia therefore went to New Zealand but despite their best efforts could not hold back the dominant Peugeot driver. Alen was second.

It was only to be expected that this produced a mixed reaction. Those manufacturers who had committed themselves heavily to Group B were not best pleased. From some there was even talk of legal action. Others, those with a big production output to fall back on, were inclined to favour the changes and among the press there was general support, the feeling being that without profound revisions World Championship level rallying would become another version of Formula One, only more dangerous.

Lancia's Cesare Fiorio was on the side of change. Although the company had invested much in their Group B and Group 5 cars (with a small capacity engine from Ferrari planned for the latter at one point in its development), Fiorio expressed doubts about the direction in which the force of competition was taking Lancia. He was not sure what cars

his drivers would use in the future, he said, but if there was a Championship Lancia would be in it, prepared to win.

Of course, in saying this he knew well that he reflected the views of many in Fiat, for whom rallying needed to relate to production cars. Despite his long advocacy of specially devised machines, Fiorio had built his early reputation on success with that wonderful Lancia standard, the Fulvia. He only turned to the Stratos because the rules of the game allowed him to do so. Now he would respond to different rules and naturally, since had had no other choice, the car to use had to be the 4X4 Delta, examples of which were already being seen in Group N of the prestigious Italian National Championship.

But getting the Delta ready for Group A competition in 1987 was not going to be easy. Much work was necessary, not least in the area of rule analysis as the new regulations gradually became available. Meanwhile, the '86 season had still to be completed and Lancia, having taken no points from Corsica after the team withdrew as a mark of respect to their dead colleagues, dropped to second place in the Championship. It was therefore

Three S4's went to New Zealand but despite all of their best efforts Lancia's drivers could not keep Kankkunen's Peugeot from finishing in first place.

necessary to perform well in Greece, where the 33rd Acropolis Rally was held in early June.

Three S4s were entered for the event, driven by Alen, Biasion and Mikael Ericsson, Lancia's new young Swedish driver imported from Audi. In inviting Ericsson to replace Toivonen, Fiorio revealed the shape of the 1987 team which would undoubtedly be equipped with 250bhp Deltas. With considerable Group A experience behind him, the 26-year-old was expected to respond well to the reduced power of the cars though he also proved capable of coping with Group B power when he tried the S4 for the first time at Lancia's La Mandria test track. Whether he could be wholly confident in Lancia's offer remained to be seen, however, since it was known that Fiorio had also been talking to Audi's Walter Rohrl, an old Lancia hand now without a drive following the German company's withdrawal from rallying.

In response to both FISA's rule changes and

criticism of the previous year's event, which many felt had become over-long and also less demanding, the '86 Acropolis was shortened and rerouted. Only 38 stages were planned instead of the previous year's 46, some of which had been run at night and caused much irritation. The event was to occupy only three days and the whole of the Peloponnese section vanished. It might, on paper, have seemed a milder blooding for young Ericsson than he could otherwise have expected. Unfortunately it was not the case; nor was there any relief for his more experienced colleagues and the Acropolis was the starting point for an arduous struggle for Lancia.

Only Biasion finished the rally, coming a good second to Kankkunen's Peugeot. Alen too hung on to the end but finally blew up his engine in a last desperate attempt to catch the French car. Ericsson, who performed well enough on his first Group B drive, retired after 17 stages with a shattered differential and collapsed suspension.

This result left Lancia still in second place in the Championship, 19 points behind Peugeot but well ahead of Volkswagen. In the Drivers Championship Alen lay second to Kankkunen but in neither event was the final outcome yet clear. Lancia therefore set off for New Zealand and rally number eight in the series with everything to play for. Despite the great distance and costs involved in sending the team to the other side of the world, the S4s went to the start line in Auckland on July 5th. This time all three finished but it was still Kankkunen's Peugeot that took first place, followed by Alen, Biasion and Ericsson in that order. Slowly and steadily the French team widened its lead over the Italians and a sense of desperation grew among the Lancia drivers.

Since Monaco, nothing had really gone well. Despite an accumulated 87 points the fact

In New Zealand the S4's suffered much at the hands of Kankkunen and Peugeot. The wild Group B cars had run out of time and the Finn's performance for the French team made him an obvious candidate for a Lancia drive in the future.

remained that the team had only one victory to its credit from five events. It was therefore a matter of great relief to most that Biasion won in Argentina, the next event in the calendar. The one who was not best pleased was Alen, who had been instructed to hold the second place he inherited on stage 15 when Kankkunen's Peugeot lost a wheel. The Finn, who needed all the points he could get in his pursuit of the Drivers Championship, felt that he should have been allowed to fight it out with Biasion for first place. But as the Italian said after the rally, 'I was in front at the time and he wasn't.'

Finland's Rally of the Thousand Lakes, held early in September, was now central to Lancia's Championship hopes, With one rally in hand over Peugeot, a win and 20 points in the north would go far. Alas, it was not to be. Although the company sent cars for Alen and Ericsson and also prised Kalle Grundel out of Ford to drive a third S4, the rally finally went Peugeot's way. Yet it was a close

Martini Lancia liveries went through various changes over the years. In the main the cars were white, with the Martini stripes variously applied from time to time. The top picture shows the S4 wearing the most usual disposition, one that transferred unchanged to the first generation of HF4WD works cars. The lower drawing illustrates the first transformation of the colour scheme.

For a brief period early in 1991 the cars wore scarlet liveries with jazzy, post modern stripes. This did not please for long and the theoretical dislocations which underlay the design were quickly abandoned in favour of a softly flowing reworking of the S4 style.

LEFT **Alen, exhaust flaming on the over run, pushes his S4 into a right hand turn during the 1986 San Remo Rally. Alen won the event, but only as a result of Peugeot's disqualification on a technicality.**

BELOW LEFT **Alen in Wales during the 86 RAC. The rally was won by Salonen in a Peugeot but Alen finished second, a result which put him one point ahead of Kankkunen in the Drivers Championship.**

run thing. Alen held the lead for much of the time, his car behaving perfectly for once, unlike those of Ericsson and Grundel, who both lost time putting damaged suspension and transmission to rights after violent collisions with the landscape. What finally put paid to Markku's chances was the unyielding pressure of Salonen and Kankkunen behind him: on the last leg, at dawn on Sunday, Alen, trying that little bit too hard, ran out of road. By the time he regained it his narrow lead over Salonen was gone and he had to be content with third place. Ericsson and Grundel finished fifth and sixth.

So that was that. Theoretically a tie was still possible, but the reality of the situation was that the 1986 World Rally Champions were Peugeot, despite there remaining a further three events to go.

The next Lancia appearance was San Remo, the Italian leg of the Championship and of great significance to the company as a consequence. It was also significant for Alen, who though lying second to Kankkunen in the Drivers Championship, still had every chance of ending the season at the head of the table. Unfortunately, although Lancia cleaned up by finishing in the first three places, the victory was pyrrhic: after a mid-rally squabble over the homologation rules, Peugeot were disqualified, leaving them leaping for their lawyers and Alen within three points of Kankkunen, but with only FISA and Fiorio to thank for it.

Peugeot took their revenge in the RAC. Salonen won but Alen was second, a result which put him one point ahead of Kankkunen. The final event of the year, the Olympus Rally in the USA, would therefore have to be contested by both drivers unless FISA made a decision on the San Remo debacle beforehand. As many expected, the bureaucrats failed once again. At a tribunal meeting held on November 23rd, only a week before the US event, no decision was reached, the matter being referred to the full FISA Executive on December 18th. There was consequently nothing for it but for Alen and Kankkunen to cross the Atlantic and fight it out in the Olympus.

In the event, Alen won. He drove well and consistently and fully deserved his victory, however long or short his reign as Champion would prove to be. He had not long to wait. Eleven days after winning the Championship Alen lost it; the San Remo result was annulled, leaving Kankkunen as World Champion Driver by 14 points. All in all, the history of Lancia's magnificent Group B rally cars did not end on a high note. Whether the company would regain its past pre-eminence in the new world of Group A remained to be seen.

6 *New wine in old bottles*

IN 1987, THIRTEEN YEARS AFTER a Fulvia last appeared in a World Championship event, Lancia again went rallying with a production car. Immediately following the Corsican tragedy and FISA's dramatic abandonment of Group B specials, Fiorio and Lombardi had begun to apply themselves to the problems of making the conservative, respectable Delta into a future champion. Altogether, it took a little over six months. While others grumbled and scratched their heads, Lancia and their chums at Abarth just got on with it. They wasted no time lamenting the loss of their glamorous supercars. Just as the Stratos and its progeny were built to exploit the rules, now that those rules had changed again so the Group B cars became part of history. Italians are pragmatic and Lancia is a very Italian company.

Development of a production four wheel drive system had been in hand at Lancia since 1982, when they showed the prototype Delta 4X4. Work

ABOVE **Announced at the same time as the Delta HF4WD, the Prisma 4WD actually appeared on the market first. The Prisma's commercial appeal was considerably enhanced by this move.**

LEFT **The HF4WD was announced at the 1986 Turin Salon. It arrived on the scene at a most opportune moment, providing Lancia with the ideal Group A machine at a time when their opponents had nothing comparable to fall back on following the FISA decision to outlaw Group B.**

on this project had been continuous since then and company announcements in 1985 suggested that a production version would be ready by the end of the year. Much of the research carried out on the S4 had also been fed into this development and it was a sad coincidence that with the anticipated production date delayed, Toivonen's death and the immediate Group B ban occurred at the very time Lancia finally announced two new production 4X4's at the 1986 Turin Salon.

Bitter though this coincidence was, it is hardly surprising that Fiorio immediately recognised the opportunity presented to Lancia by a new car and

the shift to Group A rallying. It also explained some of Peugeot's pique and their legal action against FISA, for the truth was that the S4 Delta had not been doing too well against Peugeot's devastating 205 Turbo. Jean Todt, the French team's manager, had expected to maintain this advantage in the coming season but when his cars were outlawed he had to face the fact that while Peugeot had no suitable production car to take its place, his Italian rivals were very well provided for.

The first production 4WD Lancia to go on sale, however, was not a Delta but a Prisma. As part of Lancia's total revamp of its medium capacity models, the 4WD Prisma became the new, top of the range, middleweight sedan. Billed as Italy's first four wheel drive saloon, the new version had a 2 litre 115 CV injection engine fitted with the latest Weber-Marelli electronic engine management system. The transmission, which owed much to the collaboration of Steyr-Puch, used an epicyclic central differential joined to a Ferguson viscous coupling. Cosmetically this comfortable, well appointed sedan differed from its front drive siblings in having a redesigned bonnet and head lamps and a deeper ventilation grille set below the bumper.

LEFT **In 1987 the Delta range was relaunched. The potential to be derived from World Championship victories with the car inspired Lancia to offer seven refreshed models at the '86 Turin Show, including among them the GTie shown here.**

RIGHT **The various external and internal styling changes made to the 4WD considerably enhanced its sales appeal. Visually, the adoption of round headlights in place of single square lamps gave the car a seriously sporting image, while the retrimmed and reshaped seats provided driver and passengers with a comfortable, habitable environment from which to enjoy its performance.**

BELOW **The centre piece of the relaunch was, of course, the HF4WD. Every opportunity was taken to emphasise that buyers of the car were getting into a hot shot machine which, with certain adaptations, was a real World Champion. In this implication, Lancia's publicists were in no way guilty of exaggeration.**

Other Prisma models were also reworked. The 1300 was given a breakerless ignition system; the 1.5 adopted a Digiplex controller and both received new, twin choke carburettors fitted with fuel cut off systems. A new 1.6 litre injection version was also introduced which used the 1AW Weber-Marelli injection/ignition controller fitted to the 4WD and shared the redesigned fascia, instruments and interior given to all of the new range.

The Delta itself, not unnaturally, also underwent a similar revivification. After seven years on the market a relaunch had been decided upon, a necessary move suddenly given additional, unexpected impetus by the car's impending debut on the World Rally Championship stage. Lancia showed seven different models at the Turin Show, four of which were normally aspirated and three with turbochargers. Customers for the Delta were

thus able to choose from the 1.3, the 1.3LX, the 1.5 automatic, the GTie, the HF Turbo, the HF4WD and the Turbo DS diesel. Of these, only the HF4WD and Turbo DS were genuinely new. Or newish: the diesel got its motor from the Prisma and the 4X4 took the Thema 2 litre engine and

RIGHT **In the opinion of many knowledgeable observers the 1.6ie Delta engine offered the ideal combination of performance, economy and mechanical quality. The GT, in which this engine was used, was to some extent overshadowed by the HF and the 4WD but in many ways it was just as desirable a car. In fact, for everyday motoring it was probably better.**

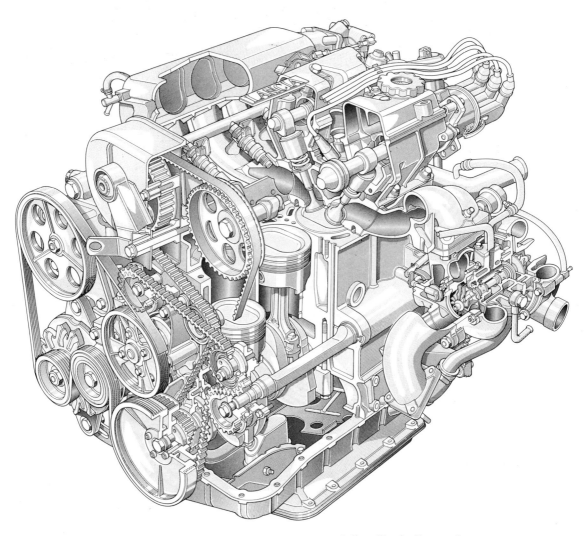

ABOVE **2-litre Turbo Integrale.**

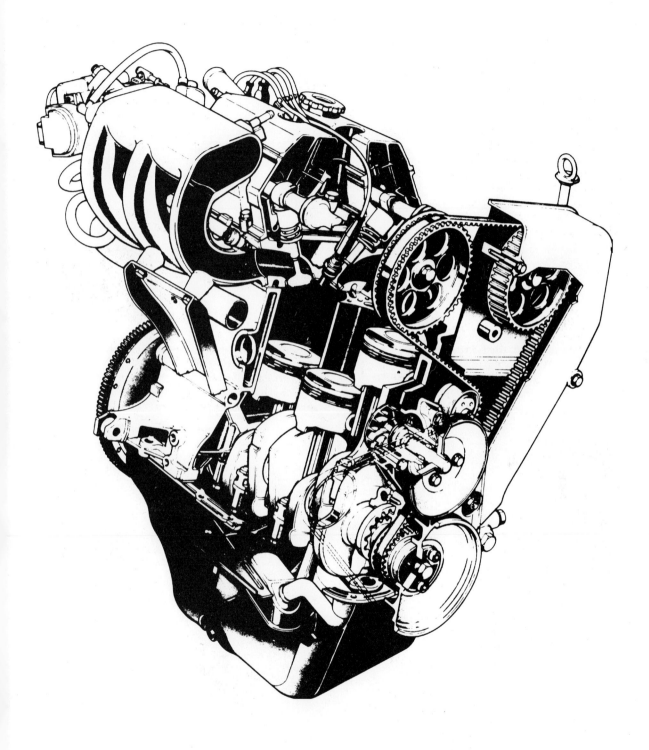

ABOVE **On the road, the GTie was a driver's car in every way. With 108bhp available at 5900rpm it had a top speed of 185kph (175 with catalytic converter). More importantly, it had a chassis well able to deal with this performance.**

BELOW **Off the road, of course, it could not compete with the 4WD. Total traction offered drivers considerable security on unstable surfaces which, in road terms meant rain, snow and ice and, on occasions, the beach.**

ABOVE **The Turbo Diesel Delta appealed to an entirely different section of the market from the HF and 4WD. Nevertheless, it was still a sprightly performer with a top speed of 170kph indicating the way forward for diesel power.**

BELOW **Top speed for the Integrale, seen here in typically loose promotional conditions, was 215kph. The 2litre, 185bhp motor was a delight and coupled to the best production 4WD system on the market.**

Architecture and automobiles (and girls) are necessary companions in the eyes of Italian photographers and publicists. Yet the influence of one upon the other is more than passing.

Giugiaro's design owes something to those Italian 'designers' such as Brunelleschi and Alberti, who transformed the Gothic through the resurrection of Classicism.

ABOVE **Digital Delta. Technological advance within Lancia contributed to the dominance of the Group A Delta, ensuring its place at the head of the World Championship table in a way which caused great frustration to its rivals.**

Prisma 4WD transmission, though with a Torsen (torque sensing) rear differential. Not that this was any criticism of the company. Good design often springs from the innovative combination of existing material and, in the case of the HF4WD, the combination proved electrifying.

While all of the latest Deltas benefited from the major reworking (which, in detail, reflected the changes made to the Prisma) the new 4X4 was a significant advance: as soon as it got into the hands of the testers it was clear that Lancia had a hit on their hands. By coupling the wonderful 8 valve Thema turbo 2 litre engine's 165 CV to a well conceived and executed four wheel drive system, the Turin designers set new standards of excellence for total traction and were instantly rewarded by glowing press reports.

In many respects it was the engine as much as the transmission that improved the car. Unlike the smaller, FWD Deltas, which sometimes seemed mechanically harsh, the 4X4 had a smooth, unburstable feel to it. Much of this sense came from the balancing shafts incorporated into the engine but was emphasised by the overboost provided by the Garrett T3 turbocharger. Floor the acceleration and momentarily the wastegate ceased to drain power, sending the car surging forward in a breathtaking way which, when tied to the total traction and stability of the transmission, could become dangerously addictive. Very few experienced drivers who tested the car had anything but praise for it. Even those who were sceptical about total traction's benefits on dry roads were converted by the Delta. And in the wet there were no doubters.

Having such a car about to go into full scale production at the time the rule changes were announced was a great relief to Fiorio and Lombardi. Although neither was deluded about the amount of work needed to bring the car to competition standard, both were optimistic. After all, none of their competitors were better placed. Only

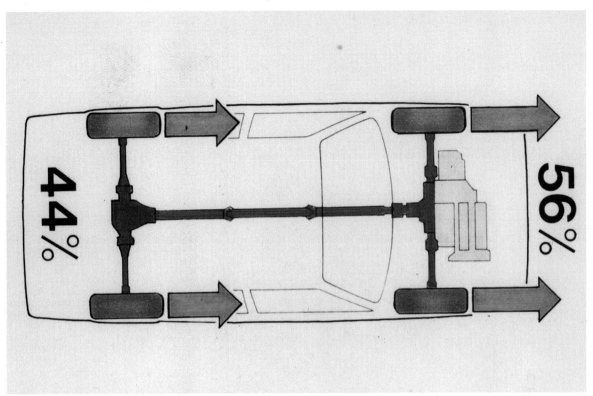

ABOVE LEFT **The Turbo Diesel engine, fitted to both the Delta and the Prisma, used a Bosch VE injection system with a KKK turbocharger and intercooler. It produced 80bhp at 4200rpm and developed 17.5kgm of torque at 2400rpm. It was Lancia's first small capacity diesel, though they had half a century's experience of big commercials.**

BELOW LEFT **Prisma 4WD mechanicals. The 2Litre engine, derived from the Thema, was also used in the Delta but the Prisma's transmission differed in having an epicyclic centre differential coupled to a selectable Ferguson rear differential. The Delta was fitted with an automatic Torsen system.**

ABOVE **Initial power split on the 4×4 was set at 58/42% front and rear. During the car's gestation various proportions were tried but the balance was finally set at 56% front and 44% rear.**

Mazda, perhaps, with the 323 Turbo 4X4 was a potential rival. With its 1.6 litre 16 valve engine, capable of producing some 248bhp, the Japanese car had a useful power advantage over the Lancia. What it lacked was the sophistication of the Delta's four wheel drive system and the sheer rally nous of Fiorio and Lombardi behind it.

These two surveyed their rivals carefully. Ford was in a cleft stick. It had a good 4X4 system in an underpowered chassis and a powerful Cosworth engine in a rear wheel drive car. Neither option looked good and since the Group A regulations required a minimum production of 5000 vehicles each year for homologation purposes, Ford could not get a hybrid into production in time. Audi, too, were stuck. Only the 200 Quattro held promise and in the end it was to prove uncompetitive. Among the other factories there were none capable of coming within striking distance of Lancia.

Against this largely unprepared array, Lancia had a head start with the HF4WD. Lombardi was already well acquainted with the car, even though he had not designed it. Fiorio, recognising that Group A would be the Championship Formula for the foreseeable future, saw much benefit in it. Between them they knew that the Delta would serve their needs well, though not without considerable effort.

A start was made with a single, slightly modified car. At La Mandria, Rozagno, one of the development team, put in many hours and kilometres in a 4X4 equipped with Uno Turbo brakes, mildly tuned motor and a standard gearbox. Various proposals were made about the system of differentials and about power split, and as data accumulated Lombardi and Limone began to reach conclusions.

The Group A regulations gave considerable

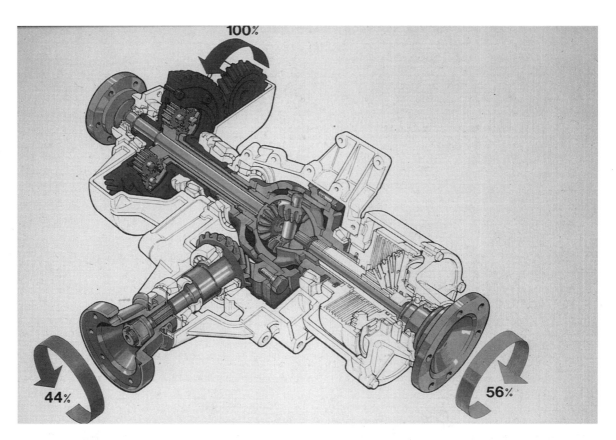

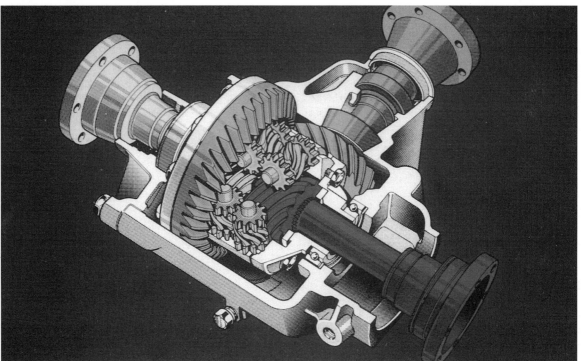

scope for development. Despite their total inflexibility about the package, they were generous about its contents. In the first place they were quite clear that the body shell had to be standard: that is, a production four seater drawn from the line. The suspension had also to conform to the standard design, as had the engine, but both these units could be improved within given limits. Engines, for example, could have redesigned cams, new pistons and valves and other modifications, including a different ignition system. Suspension components could be strengthened and adapted to meet the demands of rallying and gearboxes were also allowed to be redesigned to competition specifications.

Lombardi and his colleagues had to deal with all of this in short order. Mercifully, the car was far less complex than the S4 had been and many of the solutions to the Group B racer's problems – power split, for example – could be quickly adopted to the Group A machine. Less easily soluble were matters of engine cooling, wheel and tyre size and serviceability. In fact this last difficulty was insoluble. Production cars are not built with speed of service and component changes in mind and in the case of the Delta, chief mechanic Luigi Podda and his men simply had to learn new tricks. That they did so was eventually reflected in their ability to change a gearbox in half an hour, thought at first it took over twice as long.

Wheel and tyre size was another intractable matter. Being limited to the wheel arches of the standard body caused many headaches and led eventually to the introduction of the Integrale, with its bulges. But until such time as this evolved car became available, Lancia's drivers had to cope with less than the optimum tyre sizes on both gravel and tarmac. Nevertheless, under test they coped well. Out at La Mandria, in strict secrecy, Lombardi's testers got the car to within seconds of S4 lap times. On gravel, under certain circumstances the times

ABOVE LEFT **Delta 4x4. Front wheels drove on one side through an epicyclic gear set and on the other through a viscous coupling. Drive was taken to the rear wheels through a light, split propeller shaft. The prototype and later the Prisma had a manual lock out on the rear differential.**

LEFT **The Delta rear differential operated through an automatic Torsen system which used twin crown wheels and helical planetary gears engaged with the half shaft worm gears.**

were virtually the same. What told against the less powerful cars, of course, was straight line speed and acceleration which, for the Group B machines, approached Formula One standards. On the other hand, proper development of the Delta's transmission and suspension would more than compensate for this and Lombardi and his team hoped to bring the '87 Group A cars up to and beyond Group B standards in short order.

The cars that were finally handed over to the works drivers for acclimatisation and fine tuning were a real advance on the production model. At Abarth the bare shells delivered from the Chivasso factory had been strengthened with additional welds and fitted with full roll cages designed for torsional strength as well as driver protection, making the cars at least twice as stiff as normal, though still less rugged than the S4. New, specially constructed suspension components were fitted carrying different wheels and tyres. Brembo brakes were added, the gearbox was reconstructed and the standard engine replaced with a full house 240bhp motor. Fortunately, the one area where nothing had to be radically changed was the transmission. Over the years, Lancia had developed the most sophisticated all-wheel-drive package available, one that benefited much from the S4's competitive history. The Group A cars therefore had a competition-devised system from the first, though in layout the Delta 4X4 and the S4 differed considerably. In the case of the S4, which was mid-engined, the gearbox and centre differential lay in the middle of the car. However, the Delta, with its front wheel drive provenance had its gearbox integral with the engine. Lancia's engineers therefore put the 'centre' differential at the front, driving the wheels through a Ferguson viscous coupling on one side and an epicyclic gear set on the other.

The power split was set at 56% front–44% at the back, with the rear wheels driven through a Torsen differential. This device sensed the grip at each wheel and sent power to where it was of most use through a clever system of twin crown wheels and helical planetary gears engaged in the worm gears on each half shaft. All most complex but effective.

Painted white, with the usual Martini stripes fore and aft, the 1120kg cars (only 70kg lighter than the road going 4X4) were as far removed from the distinctive, bizarre S4 as could be imagined and Biasion's first reaction to driving one was to say, 'Well, now we are reduced to low powered cars, eh?' Such a response was hardly surprising. After the race car power and performance of the Group B specials, Group A must have seemed tame at first. Yet,

Engineers Pianta (right) and Petronio in conversation. Giorgio Pianta has been responsible for the development testing of many competition Lancias and contributed much to the new Group A 4WD Delta.

whatever disappointment the drivers may have initially felt was soon dispelled by the sheer character and quality of the 4X4 which, when all was said and done, was every bit as powerful, nimble and fast as the Stratos, still considered by many to be the greatest ever rally car.

Testing proper began in August 1986. By October cars were in Elba being put through their paces by Pianta and some of the works drivers; and at San Remo, on October 13th, the Group A Delta was publicly unveiled to the press in the gardens of the Royal Hotel. An homologation date was set for December and the rush was on to get cars ready for the first event of 1987, the Monte Carlo Rally.

Given Lancia's previous difficulties in meeting their homologation deadlines, considerable scepticism existed among their rivals about the December announcement. After all, the regulations required 5000 appropriate vehicles to have been produced and Lancia had already failed to get the HF4WD to the Frankfurt Show in 1985, as was promised. Still, there were ways and means. When the homologation date arrived and FISA found that Lancia, as predicted, had failed to complete 5000 identical vehicles, they invoked the notion of 'honourable intent': that is, Lancia intended to build the required number but had not managed to do so. Quite how honourable the actual intent was raised doubts. Although FISA's inspectors had actually found evidence of the required number of cars, they had been shown 3,200 with standard Garrett turbos and another 1,900 with KKK's. Nevertheless, provisional homologation was given, provided the KKK turbos vanished. They could run in the Monte, FISA said, and if 5000 Garrett-equipped cars appeared by mid February, everything would be fine. Ah well, rule bending has a long history in motor sport.

As well as matters mechanical, Fiorio also had to contend with the question of who would drive the cars once they got to the start line. Much speculation had appeared in the Italian motoring press during the autumn and the names of Rohrl and Kankkunen occurred often, together with rumours that Alen might finally depart in the direction of another team. Such conjectures, the stuff of Italian motor sport, were finally quelled by Fiorio just before the San Remo rally, when he announced that Alen and Biasion would represent Lancia in 1987, joined in all probability by Kankkunen: which was how it transpired.

Junior team membership was also being negotiated. The Jolly Club, under Totip Colours, would contest Group N in appropriate events with Delta's driven by Alessandro Fiorio and Michele Ragueri and it was likely that the well-known Grifone team would also run semi works HF4WD cars.

Final preparation for the 1987 season took place in a rush on top of the Great St. Bernard. Once snow had closed the Pass, Lancia negotiated access with the appropriate – and willing – authorities and spent hectic days in fine tuning and practice for what was to prove a snowy first round.

For various reasons, which included the sheer stress of continuous competition, Alen was rested for the Monte, his place being taken by the French driver, Bruno Saby. Even the most competent and dedicated of professionals found the virtually incessant round of rallying exhausting and, despite having less powerful cars to drive, a break was necessary. That it took the form of a busman's holiday was perhaps no surprise to Alen, who found himself drawn into Giorgio Pianta's Scandinavian winter testing of the Delta, prior to the Swedish Rally. Some rest.

7   The reprieve

IN MANY WAYS the heavy snow which characterised the '87 Monte was a promotional bonus. It evened things up between what the Group A cars could do and what would have been expected from Group B. As it happened, some Group B cars smaller than 1600cc did run, though only after intervention by FISA with instructions to the organisers, who had originally banned them, perhaps through fear of

Frenchman Bruno Saby on snow during the 1987 Monte Carlo Rally. Heavy snow that year helped the new Lancias to victory, but their success was marred by unproven accusations of turbo twisting. Saby retired.

contamination by association with their banished brothers.

The three Lancias that took the start on January 17th quickly silenced the Jeremiahs who predicted the end of high speed rallying with the passing of what the Italians called 'the monsters'. In fact the Deltas were so fast they aroused instant suspicions that they were illegal. Over the initial stages they simply left the opposition behind, leading to gossip that they were running with KKK turbos, capable of adding at least another 25bhp to the 250 output of Garrett blown engines. Lancia's reported behaviour out on the road seemed to confirm that something was amiss. The *Motor Sport* correspon-

dent described them as highly secretive and aggressive at service points; an Audi team member fell foul of mechanics and minders when he produced a camera. No action was taken by anyone at this stage, however, and the Lancia drivers continued to assert themselves. Biasion and Saby made all the running at first. Kankkunen, new to the car, took his time initially but soon moved into contention. When Saby retired with a broken gearbox on Stage II, east of Aubenas, where there had been an overnight stop, the World Champion took the lead.

Unfortunately he was unused to Lancia's traditional team management of results. Fiorio had decided early on that Biasion should win. The reason was fairly clear. In Italian eyes the Monte Carlo is still the most important rally to win, and for Lancia it was therefore equally important that their

Juha Kankkunen, new to Lancia and to the Delta, led the '87 Monte until the end, when team orders required him to give way to his Italian team mate, Mikki Biasion.

winning car should be driven by an Italian. It was duly announced that to avoid an unnecessary clash between the two leading drivers, the result would be decided in favour of the fastest driver over the Burzet stage. This turned out to be Biasion.

Nevertheless, when he arrived at the start of the final stage, Kankkunen found himself in the lead by two minutes, time he was instructed to lose before the end. Unable or unwilling to do so, he simply got to within 100 metres of the finish and stopped, only going on when Biasion had taken first place.

Lancia duly collected their 20 points and Biasion, perhaps with mixed feelings, collected his. Kankkunen, new to Italian rallying but wholly professional, accepted his 15 points and said nothing. But others were less inclined to hold their tongues and Achim Warmbold, Mazda's team manager, lodged a formal protest about alleged breaches of homologation by the winning Lancias. Warmbould had been one of those who, from the first, had openly doubted the Delta's legitimacy on the grounds of its speed. He and others had speculated that in some way the car's power output was close to or beyond the FISA limit of 300bhp – a seemingly fanciful notion in every way, exept to those who knew the ins and outs of big business rallying. The substance of his formal complaint, however, centred on ventilation holes in the front that did not appear on the Group N cars and extra bracing

Sweden had seldom been successful for the Turin cars but in 1987 they briefly won when Ericsson, who finished second on the road, was given first place following the temporary disqualification of the winning Mazda.

to the rear suspension. At the post-rally inspection the winning cars were closely examined by FISA engineers. After careful consideration of the Group A rules it was agreed that the Lancias conformed in every way. Warmbold's protest was dismissed.

With their first and second places confirmed and with first place in Group N also under their belts as a result of 11th place overall by Bertrand Balas and Eric Lane in a French, Gaultier-sponsored car, the Lancia team returned to Turin briefly, before setting off to Scandinavia for the Swedish Rally.

This northern event was not one of Lancia's

best. For a few years it had been excluded from the World Championship and Lancia had ignored it. Not since 1975, when Waldegaard and Thorszelius won with the Stratos, had the team taken 20 points from what many considered to be the classic winter rally: but now, flushed with their Monte victory and with an ideal car, they sought to repeat that old victory.

Three entries were made for new, unrallied Deltas registered as TO66484F, TO66485F and TO66486F, driven respectively by Alen, Kankkunen and Mikael Ericsson. With a bare three weeks between Monaco and Karlstad, Lombardi and his engineers had little enough time for the specific preparation of what were still new and

LEFT **Markku Alen was was Lancia's most loyal and long standing driver. He joined the team from Fiat in 1974, at the end of the Fulvia era, and went on to win World Championship events in all of the great Lancias – Stratos, 037, S4 and Delta. He moved to Subaru in 1991.**

BELOW **Juha Kankkunen joined Lancia in 1987 after a successful period with Peugeot. The Delta, particular the later Integrale, suited his style well.**

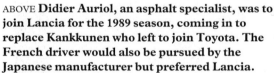

ABOVE **Didier Auriol, an asphalt specialist, was to join Lancia for the 1989 season, coming in to replace Kankkunen who left to join Toyota. The French driver would also be pursued by the Japanese manufacturer but preferred Lancia.**

LEFT **Ericsson, (right) and Bilstam, joined Lancia from Audi soon after Toivonen's death. Mikael Ericsson quickly learned to cope with the power of the S4 but Fiorio's motives in bringing him into the team lay in the future and Group A.**

Daniel Cerrato made frequent appearances for Lancia but was often found behind the wheel of a Totip or Fina car as well as part of the Martini team.

largely untried cars. Pianta's Swedish testing in early January and some previous work done in Finland during December was of great value, but there still remained so much to do. It was the price paid for bringing a new car forward in a rush. Development that ran parallel to competition was always fragmented and fraught with difficulties. There was never enough time to pull cars, engineers and drivers out of the hurly burly of the rally season in order that careful, considered testing could be done. That teams like Lancia managed to do as much as they did was utterly remarkable.

Because of early snowfall in Sweden, all of the teams entered in the '87 rally hoped for good, hard packed surfaces on which to drive. Unfortunately for Kankkunen, who started number one, that early snow was added to by fresh falls when he got away from Karlstad on the first Etape. This slowed him down, turning him into a snow plough for later starters and somehow established the tenor of Lancia's rally from the beginning.

Alen and Ericsson, starting 4 and 8 respectively, gained some consequent advantage from their team mates' predicament. Although Alen never really got going, Ericsson had a trouble free first leg, finishing at the head of the field by 14 seconds. This situation was not to last, however. Changed weather conditions on the second day enabled Salonen, in an improved and revitalised Mazda 323 Turbo 4WD, to assert himself. With Alen the

ABOVE **1987 Portuguese Rally. Kankkunen's car (number 1) receives attention and a tyre change at a service point. A shorter and softer rally after the tragedy of 1987.**

BELOW **Under African skies. Vic Preston (Jnr.), a long term Safari Rally expert and regular backup driver for Lancia, takes a rail crossing in the '87 East African event.**

Yves Loubet, mandatory French driver for the '87 Tour de Corse, takes his Delta Group A car along a tortuous coast road. Mercifully there were no tragedies for Lancia that year.

RIGHT **Yves Loubet joined Lancia in 1987, having previously developed his skills on Alfas and BMWs. He had a particularly fine record in the Tour de Corse.**

frustrated victim of various mechanical faults and Kankkunen and Ericsson losing time during servicing, he took the Japanese car to the front to win from Ericsson by 23 seconds. Warmbold's revenge was sweet.

It was also short lived. For reasons best known to themselves, FISA stepped in to challenge the result. Throughout the rally the Federation's technical director, Gabriel Cadringher, and a small team of engineers had been conducting spot checks on cars. Suddenly, at the end of the event, they declared the result provisional until certain technical aspects of the Mazda were checked out. Their concern seemed to centre on the new turbocharger fitted to the car. This ultimately turned out to be legitimate but at the time the homologation document suggested otherwise, to the possible glee of Lancia who had, of course, suffered at Wormbold's hands in Monaco.

Up to this point the World Championship had not bared its teeth. The Monte and the Swedish, though demanding, were not car breakers. Those who were critical of the abolition of Group B and had, from the beginning, cast doubt on the strength of Group A cars as front line championship contenders therefore remained sceptical. They pointed to the structural limitations of the production car and to the limited suspension reinforcement allowed by the regulations. With the advent of round three, the Portuguese Rally, they all expected their reservations to be confirmed.

After the tragedy of the 1986 rally, when spectators were killed, and the works drivers withdrew *en masse*, the organisers removed the risky Sintra stages. In their place they re-adopted the previous practice of using the race circuit in Estoril for the opening tests. They also went to considerable effort to ensure that spectators and cars were kept separate, efforts which, unfortunately, were confounded by yet another death before the rally ended.

Compliance with FISA's new regulations meant that the 20th Portuguese Rally was shortened, both in distance and in the number of stages, which were reduced to 37 from the previous number of 46 or 47. This brought the overall distance down to 2088kms, though in terms of rigour the loss of a mere 280kms from the 1986 distance did nothing to lessen the impact on the cars. The Portuguese

ABOVE RIGHT **Mikael Ericsson drove the '87 Acropolis Rally under Totip colours. The Martini cars were driven by Alen, Biasion and Kankkunen. Alen won, after another team decision which restrained his Finnish colleague.**

RIGHT **One month after the Greek event, Kankkunen found himself benefitting from the team game when he won the Olympus Rally in the States. Biasion, in command, suffered a minor delay at the point when Fiorio decided the final order, which gave the event to Kankkunen.**

Rally, as ever, was rough.

For Lancia it was the rally of the shock absorbers. So much damage was inflicted on the dampers that, at one point, the service crews ran out of replacements. New supplies were flown in from Turin but for a short while Alen, the eventual winner, had to drive defensively to avoid smashing the last usable set.

The event tested the durability of all the front

running cars. Lancia and Mazda suffered equally, though differently. The principal weakness of the Japanese cars lay in the transmission and in the cooling department. All of the Lancias had damaged shock absorbers and Biasion suffered a jammed gearbox among other delaying problems.

Despite his difficulties, which ultimately put him back to 8th position, Biasion performed well enough to win more special stages than anyone else. Alen, who was finally able to extend his lead during the last stages, once the new dampers had arrived, was second with 9 firsts to his team mate's 13. Kankkunen, the other Lancia driver, had his own share of problems but eventually finished in fourth place overall, behind Kenneth Eriksson's VW and Jean Ragnotti's Renault 11 Turbo. The final results therefore kept Lancia at the head of the Championship and Kankkunen in the lead amongst the drivers.

Some of the difficulties anticipated by Lombardi when he and Limone first contemplated the use of the Delta 4WD in serious international competition were shown up by the Portuguese Rally. That the Safari, the next event in the calendar, would reveal even more shortcomings was never in doubt. In large part the limitations of the car derived from the lack of space under the wheel arches, necessary to accommodate the range of wheel and tyre sizes and to achieve the maximum suspension travel. Each rally required something different. Portugal called for the biggest possible brakes, together with tyres deep enough to cope with rocks: the Safari, on the other hand, made less demands on brakes but needed lots of wheel travel, engine and driver cooling and effective means of keeping the dust out today and coping with mud tomorrow. The rally engineer's lot was not a happy one, and Lancia's limited involvement with the Kenyan event in 1987 probably had much to do with unsolved technical matters.

Even so, the event could not go uncontested. Lancia may not have done so well as they would have wished in past Safaris, but their commitment to it amounted to fascination. They therefore sent

one car and a support crew for their old retainer, the Kenyan driver Vic Preston junior, and another experienced local rallyist who was already campaigning his own private Delta 4WD in Kenyan events.

Some weeks before the rally a practice car was sent out, together with Maurizio Ravaglia, a journalist from the Italian magazine *Autosprint*. The testing he witnessed proved wholly successful and it seemed that the Delta, fitted up with the usual African protection of bars, vents and heat shields, might perform well. As things turned out, these hopes were dashed by major transmission failures. In a rally dominated initially by Ford then Toyota, the sole Lancia was never in contention. Eventual victory went to Audi's Hannu Mikkola, who became the first ever driver to win the Safari in a four wheel drive vehicle. Preston finished 14th.

Lancia's reduced presence in Kenya enabled the team to spend longer than usual in getting their cars ready for round five, the Tour de Corse. With the two previous Corsican rallies ending tragically for the Turin team, their preparation for this, the 31st event, was most fastidious. In many ways it was the ideal event for Lancia, one suited to the sort of cars the company had always built, where dynamic excellence and precision counted most. In fact, of the 12 Corsican events prior to 1987, Lancia had won seven and they consequently entered the latest rally determined to add to their record.

Since the main reason for going rallying at all was publicity and sales, Lancia would, when appropriate, choose crews with a particular national flavour. For the French island venue, two of the three Deltas were manned by Frenchman Saby/Fauchille and Loubet/Vieo, with Biasion/Siviero from among the regular squad. Loubet, new to Lancia, was an old hand at the Tour. In previous years he had successfully competed in an Alfa RTV6, moving up from 10th in 1984 to 3rd in 1986. Now, with the Lancia, he hoped for and achieved a better result, finishing a fine second to the winning BMW M3 of his countryman, Bernard Beguin.

Beguin's victory was a considerable achievement. BMW were not formally involved with World Rallying and the Frenchman's M3 was privately entered under Rothman colours. In the early stages of the rally Beguin took the lead but after heavy rain was forced to relinquish it to Loubet, whose Lancia, on appropriate tyres, had moved ahead of the German car by the end of the first etape. Next day, after leaving Bastia in the north of the island on dry roads, Beguin moved back into the lead. Bruno Saby, Lancia's fastest driver on the

ABOVE LEFT **Group A bell housing awaiting installation during the Olympus Rally. Lancia were seldom short of spare parts when rallying.**

LEFT **Same event, different bits. A spare engine sits on its pallet in case of need.**

Interior of one of the works cars used in the American event. Note fancy steering wheel and clean, workmanlike presentation. Everything shipshape and Bristol fashion.

day, then overdid things and was forced out with a damaged differential. Loubet and Biasion, meanwhile, stayed up with the leader to finish a satisfactory second and third. The resulting points put Lancia even further ahead in the Championship and moved Biasion into second place in the Drivers competition, a mere two points behind his team mate Kankkunen.

While all this had been going on, certain changes were taking place back at base. Conny Isemburg came in as team manager and Nini Russo took over semi official works client support. 'Lele' Pinto, a

past member of both Lancia and Fiat's World Championship squads in the days of HF Squadra Corse, joined Abarth as Head of Development in place of Giorgio Pianta, who moved to Alfa Romeo. Pinto, who had successfully rallied Fulvias, 124's, Stratos and 131's, was a useful addition to the team for he brought with him considerable experience, particularly of ice driving. As a director of the Ice School at Sestriere, a senior instructor at the Italian National Rally School and a tester with Ferrari, all of which work he continued to undertake in addition to his Abarth responsibilities, Pinto's knowledge of rally car development was vast and the Delta and its drivers gained much from his presence. In fact, before formally joining Abarth, he was already undertaking tests in Greece in company with Markku Alen who, rested for Corsica, approached the impending Acropolis Rally in a

**Lancia's photographers love snow and ice for
Integrale portraits.**

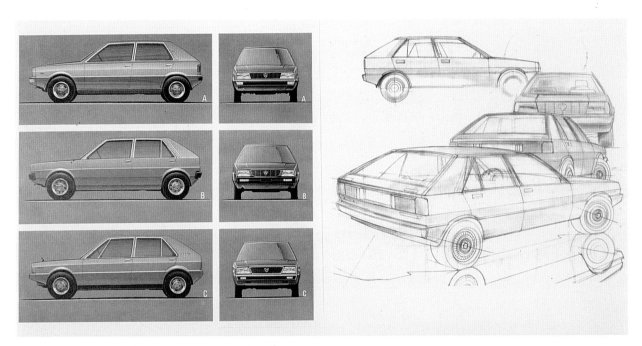

TOP **Initial sketches show Golf provenance. Various detailing alternatives illustrate how the visual appearance of a single shape is changed by minor alterations.**

ABOVE **Giugiaro's full size clay mock up revealed a simple, unpretentious shape, wholly in keeping with Lancia's conservative philosophy of design.**

**ECV2, the second generation Lancia/Fiat
experimental composite vehicle, would have
been a formidable Group S Rally car, had it not
died with the Group B collapse.**

TOP **The roadgoing S4, built for homologation purposes, was a wonderful, utterly idiosyncratic car of great rarity.**

ABOVE **ECV1. This first version of the Lancia Group S car looked much more like the S4 Delta than its successor, ECV2.**

TOP **The short lived, jazzy, red livery which the 16v Integrale's wore briefly in 1990.**

ABOVE **The old Abarth factory in Turin's Corso Marche houses the Lancia team. Its rally cars are built there from shells drawn from the production line in batches.**

TOP **The first 4 × 4 Delta Turbo prototype was a remarkably well prepared car, which generated much enthusiasm, despite a tendency towards understeer.**

ABOVE **Biasion modified his S4 to no good effect during the 1986 Monte Carlo Rally.**

TOP **Toivonen led the 1986 Swedish Rally for most of the event, only dropping out when his S4 dropped a valve on stage 13.**

ABOVE **The 1986 Acropolis Rally was a sad event for Lancia, who sent S4's for Alen (seen here), Biasion and Ericsson despite the tragedy of Toivonen and Cresto's deaths in the Tour de Corse.**

**Alessandrini, in a privately sponsored S4,
supported Alen in America in '86. Alen won and
was World Champion for eleven days.**

TOP **New Zealand '86. Alen's S4 in the Parc Fermé at the end of the first leg. The Finn eventually finished second.**

ABOVE **A Totip S4 raising the dust during the '86 Costa Smeralda rally.**

**Portugal, 1987, was overwhelmed with works
Lancias. The company supported 11 cars in total.
Alen, seen here, finished 6th.**

TOP **Alessandrini took the Sitma sponsored S4 on to the famous Pikes Peak hill climb after contesting the 1987 Olympus Rally in the USA.**

ABOVE **Tabaton, driving a Jolly Club car, shared Lancia's continued dominance of the San Remo, one of the stream of events which fell to the Delta in 1987.**

Lancia's service crews have always been of the highest calibre. Here, one of the Totip Delta's receives attention during the 1988 Portuguese Rally.

With all four feet off the ground, Loubet forces the Integrale towards 2nd place in the 1988 Tour de Corse.

Alessandri again, this time in the Sitma sponsored HF 4 × 4 during the '86 Acropolis Rally.

TOP **Let them be left, wildness and wet: mud, Safari, Fiorio, 1989.**

ABOVE **Lancia, with a 64 point lead over Toyota, went to Argentina alone. Ericsson takes a water splash on his way to a surprise victory.**

TOP **With Biasion and Fiorio retired it was left to Kankkunen to salvage 2nd place in the 1990 Safari Rally. Service became more vital than ever in appalling conditions brought on by heavy rain.**

ABOVE **After several dry rallies, the Safari reverted to form in 1990. Here Kankkunen charges a swollen, muddy river. His team mates, Biasion and Fiorio, both went out with mechanical failure.**

TOP **Didier Auriol, 3rd place man in Argentina in 1990, struggled back into contention after a plague of engine problems early in the rally.**

ABOVE **Lancia, already 1990 World Champions, had no need to contest the RAC Rally that year. That they sent cars for Biasion (seen here), Kankkunen and Auriol showed their sensitivity to criticism after failing to appear in '89.**

TOP **Bruno Saby in a Fina Integrale during the 1991 Monte Carlo Rally. Sainz, in a Toyota, was the winner.**

ABOVE **Kankkunen, ploughing, on the slippery, loose pebbles of the Australian Bush during the '91 Commonwealth Bank Rally.**

ABOVE **America again. From left to right, Kankkunen, Alen and Biasion. At this point in the 1987 season Lancia, with 114 points, were 52 points** **ahead of their nearest rivals, Audi. The Delta was beginning to demonstrate the sort of form which was to prove devastating through future seasons.**

most positive frame of mind.

At about this time work was completed on the first stage of a new performance analysis system. This took the form of an onboard computer called the 'data logger'. The instrument, weighing little more than 1kg, was fitted to the Group A Deltas to provide drivers and technicians with instant information about engine tune, gearbox performance and shock absorber action. The data accumulated in real time was recorded into tape and made instantly available for analysis at each service halt. The benefits of such precise monitoring were obvious to drivers and technicians alike, and when the system was first used in anger during the Acropolis Rally the boost given to team confidence was considerable.

Lancia's last win in Greece had been in 1983, when Walter Rohrl brought the 037 Rally into first

place. Now, with the Delta settling down as a tough, reliable and sophisticated car facing little really consistent opposition, the signs were good for a repeat performance – though hopefully not by Rohrl in the heavy 200 Quattro. It was therefore no surprise when the Lancias of Alen, Biasion and Kankkunen grabbed the first three positions quite soon after the start on May 31st. Not that they maintained their advantage for long. Although the position at the end of the first day was Biasion, Alen and Kankkunen, it had not been achieved without cost. Alen had permanently bent his car and Kankkunen was delayed by repeated punctures. Only Biasion came through relatively unscathed until being forced to drop back on day two with a defective turbo.

Prior to this, Fiorio's instructions were that the first day's order be held to the end, giving Biasion

LEFT **Although banned from international rallying, the S4 was still elegible for events such as the formidable Pikes Peak hillclimb in the USA. Here Alessandrini takes his SITMA car up the fast and tricky dirt climb.**

ABOVE **Some sense of the dramatic nature of the Argentine Rally is given by this picture of Biasion crossing a gorge during the '87 event. Biasion won, followed into second place by the Delta of Jorge Recalde.**

victory. When he was relegated and then withdrawn it was expected that Alen would be allowed to hold first position. Kankkunen, however, did not understand and set about passing his team mate, only to be ordered back by the boss. Alen, as a consequence, had an easy though possibly undeserved victory and Kankkunen no doubt resolved to quit Lancia when his contract expired.

This sort of fixing was distasteful. It had been going on for years, but that didn't make it any more

acceptable. Frequently it seemed chauvinist and although convincing commercial arguments could be put forward to mask this, the fact remained that spectators, drivers and rallying itself were ultimately short changed by the practice. It was the negation of open competition, at least in the Drivers Championship.

In terms of the World Championship itself, of course, team orders had no bearing on the legitimacy of Lancia's first and second places in the

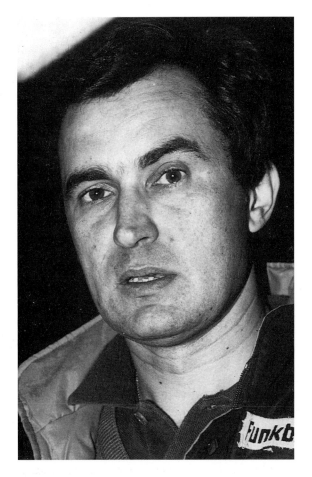

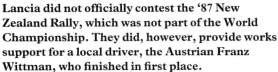

Lancia did not officially contest the '87 New Zealand Rally, which was not part of the World Championship. They did, however, provide works support for a local driver, the Austrian Franz Wittman, who finished in first place.

Jorge Recalde, an Argentinian driver of great experience, has been a regular guest in the Lancia team for several years. His experience of South American rallying has been of value in events such as the East African Safari Rally.

Acropolis. The cars and their crews clearly deserved to win. In fact, from Fiorio's point of view, to have had team members competing with one another could easily have jeopardised the final result and the additional points which put Lancia even further ahead of their nearest rival, Audi.

Fortunately for Kankkunen the practice worked in his favour one month later in America. The downbeat and poorly supported Olympus Rally held in Washington State in late June proved to be a Lancia benefit. Because of a total lack of competition, Lancia team orders, agreed in advance of the start, established that if Lancia led at halfway then team members would keep their relative positions to the end. As it happened it was Kankkunen who found himself in first place, artificially ahead of Bia-

sion, who, prior to the mid-point, had been fastest and in the lead. On Stage 24 however, under growing pressure from Kankkunen, his engine began to misfire and as he lost power and went on to three cylinders his Finnish colleague overtook him to enter the security zone of Fiorio's instructions. Biasion, his missing plug lead reconnected – for that was all that was wrong with the engine – regained the lead only to slow and hand victory to Kankkunen. Justice had reasserted itself.

It was now more than halfway through the season. Lancia, with 114 points, were 52 points ahead of their nearest rivals, Audi. The Manufacturers Championship therefore seemed secure, with only the Drivers Championship left to play for.

Lancia missed the next international rally in

New Zealand. Since it was not included in the World Championship they chose instead to support a local driver, Franz Wittman, with a works-prepared but privately financed and entered Delta. Wittman won.

The gap this opened up in the schedule before the next event, the Marlboro Rally of Argentina in early August, was welcome. Not only did it allow more time to prepare the cars for Argentina, it also enabled work to progress on the evolution Delta, the 'Tipo Z'. This latest car was not an evolution in the old Group B sense – that was not allowed for in Group A. Rather it would be produced in homologation numbers as a new model, which hopefully would be ready for FISA's approval by January 1st 1988.

Lele Pinto devoted much of his time to this car and during August ran it regularly at the La Mandria track and on the road at Vizzola Ticino. Like everyone else at Abarth, he and his colleagues were keenly aware of the distant but growing threat to Lancia from Japan and of the consequent importance of keeping the ageing HF4WD competitive. It was a serious situation, exacerbated by worries about tyres, for it seemed increasingly unlikely that Pirelli would continue to supply the team's rubber in the coming season and that a new contractor would have to be to be found. And in addition there was the small matter of drivers.

But while all this was going on Biasion and the Argentinian driver, Jorge Recalde, were notching up further points in South America. Their first and second positions secured for Lancia the World Championship for Rallies and moved Biasion in the lead in the Drivers Championship, albeit by only two points over Kankkunen. This was the quickest World Championship victory ever achieved and in some ways it rather took the heart out of the whole thing, for there still remained a further four events in the calendar. Yet it was hardly Lancia's fault. Having always placed great emphasis on the World Championship, when they found themselves with the only competitive car in Group A, they naturally made the most of it. Some benefit did come from it though, for the early victory opened up the Drivers Championship to real competition among the three leading Lancia drivers, whose order, prior to the Thousand Lakes was Biasion 1st (74 points), Kankkunen 2nd (72 points), Alen 3rd (60 points).

The World Championship for Drivers went to whoever accumulated the most points from their eight best events out of the available 13, one of which had to take place outside Europe. Lancia, for various strategic reasons, decided that each driver would contest seven rallies in total, which added a certain urgency to their efforts.

As far as possible, drivers were assigned to rallies on the basis of particular skills and national interest. Thus the Finnish round, the 37th Rally of the 1000 Lakes, appeared on Alen's and Kankkunen's list and, with the Delta 4WD now performing perfectly, one or other was likely to win on surfaces that were ideal for them and the car. Following FISA's dictates, the organisers of the event had been forced to make changes in the route. Many favourite stages from earlier years were either eliminated or modified by the introduction of detours intended to reduce average speeds. But as *Motor Sport*'s correspondent pointed out, there is no necessary connection between average speed and maximum speed, which rather undermined FISA's belief that the introduction of these changes automatically improved safety. What the route changes did produce, however, was more soft surfaces, something which added to the Delta's advantage.

From the start at Jyvaskyla it was Alen's rally. Competition from Ford, Audi and a hopefully revived Mazda team was simply not up to dealing with the Lancias, which meant that it fell to Kankkunen to make a fight of it. Earlier in the summer, in an interview with *Motor*, Kankkunen had made it very plain that the 1000 Lakes was the one rally he wanted to win. 'Nobody back home really thinks you are World Champion until you have won the 1000 Lakes', he said. Sadly, when the time came, he couldn't live up to his ambition. With Alen dominating the rally from the front, Kankkunen slid down the field as accidents and mechanical failure lost him more and more time. In struggling finally to finish fifth to Alen's first, he managed to pick up enough points to put him jointly at the head of the Championship with his Finnish team mate. He had hoped for better but certainly was not complaining. Neither was Fiorio. Lancia were piling up points and his son Alessandro, in winning the Group N competition in Finland, looked set to add yet another award to Lancia's final total.

If results now seemed predictable, San Remo, the Italian leg of the World Championship, upset everything – at least from Alen's point of view. This asphalt and gravel rally, once called the Rally of Flowers, had been the scene of many past Lancia successes. Fulvia, Stratos, 037 and S4; all had triumphed in this most prestigious Italian event. It was an Alen rally too. In the preceding 10 years the Finn had won three times, once in each car other than the Fulvia. Not unexpectedly, with this record

After a series of mishaps, including having the car's automatic fire extinguisher go off in the middle of a stage, Alen finally crashed out of the San Remo Rally on Stage 17. This effectively put paid to his Championship hopes, a particularly galling matter given his past successes in the Italian event.

behind him he approached the 1987 event with optimism. Another win and he would be clearly ahead in the championship, leaving Kankkunen and Biasion to struggle.

But it was not to be. With no team orders to contend with, Biasion made most of the running, taking first place in 20 of the 41 special stages. Alen, who punctured soon after the start, got nothing right early on, allowing Biasion and Ragnotti, in a Renault, to lead. He reasserted himself once the rally moved to Tuscany and got onto wet gravel, but to little avail. In the end, after various mishaps, which included the car's automatic fire extin-

guisher going off mid-stage, he crashed on stage 17. Biasion, meanwhile, continued to drive brilliantly, leading Bruno Saby in his Chardonnet Delta, into a wholly justified first place. In all, Delta's took seven of the first twelve places.

Biasion now led the Championship by 14 points from Alen and Kankkunen. Everything therefore depended on the RAC and on Lancia's willingness to honour the pre-season agreement restricting each driver to seven starts. Biasion, having completed his quota, was not entitled to a drive but there were many cynics abroad who reckoned he would appear. In the event they were confounded; nothing of the sort happened and it was left to Alen and Kankkunen to fight it out in an attempt to pass Biasion's total of 94 points. To do this one or other would have to win, or at least achieve second place if the palm went anywhere rather than to Lancia.

Not that there was much chance of that. Biasion and his co-driver Tiziano Siviero, who turned up to watch, knew that only extreme carelessness or bad luck would prevent one of the Finns from taking the title. The opposition provided by Ford and Audi was still inadequate and Mazda had vanished from the scene, its homologation withdrawn in November over a gearbox problem.

From the beginning it was Kankkunen's rally. No trace of tension showed as he put up a fast, faultless performance in his early duels with Alen. Both were seriously committed over the first day's sprint stages – no Mickey Mouse attitudes on this occasion – and such was Alen's determination that he rolled on a downhill at Chatsworth. Although he lost little time, it was enough to set Kankkunen clear at the end of the day, with Alen second, Ericsson, in the third works Delta, in fifth place and Russell Brookes, the English driver using a fully works-prepared but privately entered car, 10th.

Although the duel continued through the second day and the North Wales stages it was becoming clear that Kankkunen would keep a firm hold on the rally. The day ended with him still ahead of Alen, now down to third place behind Mikael Ericsson. And so it continued: even though the unpredictable could happen at any time, the feeling grew that the World Champion would retain his title and when he went into the final day with a three minute lead the matter was all but resolved. Kankkunen kept his head and his lead to the finish and the title was his. For the first time in the history of the Drivers Championship the reigning champion retained his crown.

It had been a year of great achievement for Lancia: World Rally Champions, World Drivers Championship, Group N World Rally Champions, World Champions in the shortest time and the company to have won more events in a season than any other. All this with an eight year old design.

8 Integrale

HAD IT NOT been so suddenly and successfully flung into the international rally circus, the Delta would probably have died by 1988. Eight to ten year production cycles were normal for most Lancias and by that time the car would have exhausted much of its potential. In fact, in January 1987, its likely replacement, codenamed Tipo Due, was already running around Turin under test. Lancia expected to launch this car the following year and advance promotion suggested that a 16 valve engine and permanent four wheel drive were already planned. The HF4WD prepared in 1986 might therefore have been the Delta's swansong, a resonant technical coda to a blameless life and a preview of future innovation. Yet it didn't happen that way. Becoming World Champion reprieved

the car and, as had happened with the Fulvia in the 1970's, Lancia's production plans were very quickly re-appraised.

An immediate consequence was Lombardi's recognition of the constraints imposed by the Delta's body shell on its competitive future. As a result, a second generation 4X4 was quickly acknowledged to be a necessity. Since Group A regulations required this to be a production model, the Delta range had to be further extended to include the new car, marketed as the Integrale, which, in Italian,

Flared arches front and rear, new turbocharger, uprated engine and a revised engine management programme, were all introduced to the road going Integrale as a means of improving Group A cars.

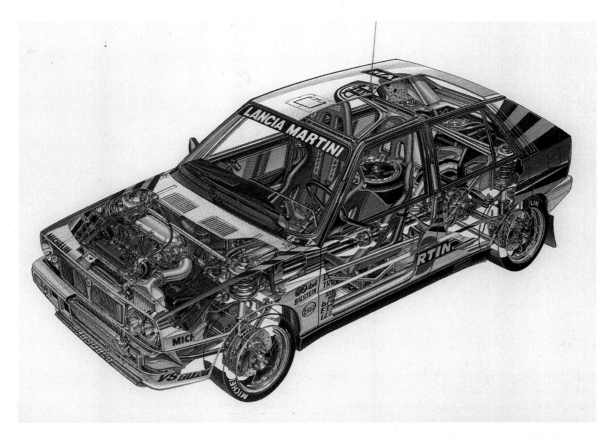

FISA introduced various modifications to the rules for the new season. In 1988 the turbo coefficient went up from 1.4 to 1.8. This enabled the Integrale to move up to the 3500cc class.

means 'whole, complete, in full'.

Promising wholeness is risky. It says that nothing is excluded. This is not to claim perfection. Rather, it claims that within given boundaries nothing relevant is omitted. The boundaries, in this case, were the Group A regulations and the vehicle designed to be successful within them. Lancia therefore committed themselves, through a name, to a machine with everything necessary to win Group A rallies. Reasons for failure were to be sought elsewhere.

It was a matter of credit to all concerned that the Integrale lived up to its name. From August 1987, prototypes were out and about around Turin and when the car was formally announced at the Frankfurt Show of that year it was enthusiastically received. Initial reports in the motoring press were immediately favourable and Lancia's market share, which had climbed rapidly on the back of their

World Championship successes, looked set for a further increase.

For it was in every way a wonderful car. On the road the Integrale added another level of experience to those established in their own time by previous Lancia revolutions. As the Lambda had shifted notions of vehicle stability in the 1920's and the Stratos added to the 1970's perception of pace and agility, so the Integrale gave the late 1980's something to think about in matters of total traction, speed and security.

It also looked the part. Without losing anything of Giugiaro's classical simplicity, the latest generation Delta added a layer of muscle, became more broad shouldered and confident. It became adult.

Visually, the car was characterised by its puffed cheeks, the stretched wheel arches designed to accommodate bigger tyres and the extended suspension travel required for rallying. It also had more holes in the front to cool the uprated 2 litre engine, which now developed 185bhp as a result of a bigger Garrett T3 turbocharger, a new intercooler, redesigned valves and revised programmes for the Weber Marelli engine management system. Per-

ABOVE **HF Turbo engine development continued steadily, making the 1.6 unit increasingly satisfying to drive. The 'Nuova' engine produced 140bhp at 5500rpm. It used a Garrett T2 watercooled turbo with max boost of 0.85 bar.**

BELOW **An increase in power for 1988 – up to a published 260bhp – a new clutch, six speed Safari gearbox, modified front suspension and 16" Speedline rims capable of taking 24/61-16 Michelin slicks for dry roads.**

ABOVE **Homologation delays kept the Integrale out of the World Championship until the Portuguese Rally. Lombardi and Lele Pinto, now in charge of development, took advantage of this to undertake additional testing.**

BELOW **The standard version of the Integrale acquired a mean black interior to go with its macho new body. All the emphasis was on power, and power dressing. And for many customers, the new look worked.**

Although the road (and river) car retained the earlier 4×4's transmission virtually intact, the Group A machines were fitted with various alternatives. These included a ZF front differential and a Ferguson replacement for the Torsen rear differential. After testing, the Ferguson system was abandoned and Torsen rear diff retained.

formance levels rose markedly, assisted by an extended overboost device which pushed pressure up to 1 bar for as long as the accelerator was hard down. A new clutch was fitted and new brakes.

Within months of coming on to the market the Integrale became the yardstick against which other four wheel drive sports cars were judged. Unfortunately, production was once again held up and the hoped-for homologation by January 1st, 1988, did not materialise. Lancia therefore began the new season with the old HF4WD. Not that it mattered. The marques and models ranged against them remained much as before. Only three different machines appeared among the 12 Group A works teams. Audi ran but one car, the 90 Quattro, instead of two; Renault and Subaru dropped out completely, to be replaced by two from Mitsubishi, with Toyota making good the Audi gap by running their Celica 2000 GT4. Numerically, then, the

competition remained the same and none of it presented a threat to Lancia.

The new season saw a number of small but useful changes to the regulations. FISA's ground rules still demanded that for homologation into Group A and Group N, cars should be four seaters produced in minimum numbers of 5000 in a twelve month period. Such modification to engine size and specification, gearbox, suspension, tyres and body as had been previously permitted remained unchanged for 1988, although additional directives

The new body style, with its well muscled shoulders and hips, gave the Integrale enormous presence. Although remaining faithful to his original design concept, Giugiaro again produced a remarkable visual change through the introduction of comparatively few new shapes.

The Group A cars weighed in at 1150kgs. with a full tank of fuel. Their new engines produced 270bhp on the road and were capable of delivering over 300bhp on the bench. The drivers found them a marked improvement on their predecessors, with Biasion describing his test car as "more of a rally car than the 4WD, nervous but pleasing, secure and not spiteful".

came into force beside them. These increased the coefficient for turbocharged engines from 1.4 to 1.7; established a new relationship between engine capacity and tyre size, required turbo cars to have intercoolers as standard, made weight relative to capacity and confirmed the power ceiling at 300bhp, irrespective of engine size. One great benefit to Lancia that followed from these directives was the opportunity to use the fattest tyres when necessary. The increased turbo coefficient moved the Delta into the under 3500cc class instead of the 3 litre group where it had previously been placed. The larger category size allowed for larger tyres, something most welcome to Fiorio and the team, which now comprised Alen, Biasion, Ericsson, Saby, Loubet, Preston and Recalde.

Unfortunately, because of the delay in getting the Integrale homologated, this change did not

Father and son – East African specialists Vic Preston Senior (left) and Junior. Preston Junior drove for Lancia in the Safari at various times, beginning with a Stratos in 1975. Prior to the '88 event he took an active part in pre-rally testing.

benefit them in the early part of the year. As it happened, Lancia were not prevented from winning the first event, the Monte, but had it not been for some misjudgement of the weather by other teams, things might have been different.

Snow seldom failed to feature in the Monegasque rally, a factor which favoured total traction and disadvantaged two wheel drive cars. The likelihood of bad weather therefore kept most of the major teams away, leaving only Mazda to compete with the Lancias in the first round of the new championship. For BMW and Ford in particular, it was a bad decision, since most of the rally was actually run under dry, snow-free conditions that would have favoured their cars. Had they appeared, the old HF4WD would have struggled, causing Fiorio and his team to lament the lack of an Integrale or two.

But luck was with them. Mazda, back in rallying after being punished by FISA for earlier gearbox transgressions, and now with Hannu Mikkola in the team, were unreliable and completely outclassed. The Lancia team of Biasion, Saby and Loubet, together with a Jolly Club car driven by

ABOVE **The Spring of 1988 saw the Integrale's first World Championship appearance. Such was Lancia's concern to do well in the Portuguese Rally that no less than eleven 4WD Deltas were on the start list. Four were Martini cars.**

BELOW **The 38th. Swedish Rally saw two Deltas competing under unusually snowless conditions. Road conditions were unpredictable and Mikael Ericsson, driving one of the two works 4WD cars, crashed and later retired.**

ABOVE **Alessandro Fiorio, son of team boss Cesare Fiorio, continued the family tradition of service to Lancia when he became a member of the works team. His grandfather, Sandro, began the tradition in the fifties when he drove a B20.**

BELOW **The Integrale's debut in Portugal resulted in a one, two, three finish for Biasion, Fiorio and Loubet. This occasioned great relief and pleasure all round, adding extra zest to the sprayed champagne.**

Alessandro Fiorio, dominated a rally characterised by a lack of works competition and a series of fine performances by privateers. Not that it was an absolute walkover. Although Saby won convincingly from Alex Fiorio, it was a privateer, Jean Pierre Ballet in a Peugeot 205 GTI, who finished third with the next Delta being the eighth placed Group N car of Giovanni del Zoppo. As for the other works cars, Biasion retired early on Stage 3 with a broken oil pump and Yves Loubet crashed on Stage 13.

Round two of the championship, the 38th Swedish Rally, saw two Martini Lancias going north to cope with more unexpected weather. With little snow, the Swedish event provided as wide a range of unpredictable road surfaces as could be imagined, which tested Michelin, Lancia's new tyre suppliers, as much as it tested Alen and Ericsson.

Lombardi, Pinto and each of the works drivers had spent time in tuning the Lancia to its new rubber. Although Pirelli still supplied tyres to the Jolly

Lancia's first ever Safari victory, long sought but always elusive, fell to Biasion and the new Integrale. The 1988 East African marathon was not without problems for the team however. At one point Biasion hit a zebra.

Club, moving to a new factory had made it impossible for them to keep up the level of supply required by the works cars. As a consequence, Lancia turned to Michelin, the French company with whom they had had a long and successful previous history. Their tyres proved to be fine but, nevertheless, it took time to acclimatise cars and drivers to their particular characteristics.

The work of tyre tuning continued in Sweden, where Mikael Ericsson contributed negatively to the process by crashing on the first special stage. Alen, more experienced and unusually cautious, ran without trouble behind the Mazdas for a while

Biasion's victory owed much to the courtesy of Mike Kirkland, a Safari rival who overlooked a breach of the regulations by Siviero, Biasion's navigator. When the car arrived at Nakuru, Siviero forgot to hand in the time card. This normally resulted in disqualification but Kirkland very graciously chose not to invoke the rules against them.

before pulling ahead, with Ericsson, once back on the road, in support. But Ericsson, who won six special stages, was not to complete the rally. His 'off' damaged the Delta's cooling system and on Stage 12 he was withdrawn when the head gasket blew. Alen, meanwhile, consolidated his lead on increasingly difficult road surfaces. 'The only thing to do was drive carefully', he said. This uncharacteristic approach paid off and Alen won by nearly two minutes from Stig Blomqvist in a works Sierra 4X4.

The tyre question that occupied much of Lancia's thinking as the Group A Integrale came slowly to fruition was a preoccupation shared throughout rallying. Michelin, with its vast experience of racing and extensive research facilities, provided

unmatched support for the Italian team in its search for ever increased performance. Tyre design and choice of tread were becoming increasingly scientific, with treads, dimensions, compounds and strength being matched to stage requirements with great precision.

All of the research and development came together in a final programme of testing during February. The Integrale's first competitive appearance had been a little earlier in the Chamonix 24 Hours Ice Race at the end of January. Driven by

Alex Fiorio drove a Totip/ Jolly Club 4WD in the '88 Swedish Rally. The conditions were more like the RAC than the usual deep Swedish snow.

To everyone's surprise, the Integrale was beaten by a Ford in the Tour de Corse. Lancia had come to consider the event their own in many ways, and giving best to Auriol's Cosworth, albeit as the result of gearbox failure on Loubet's car, was disconcerting. Here, Bruno Saby negotiates a mountain road in mist.

Formula One driver Jaques Lafitte, the car finished third. Subsequently, with homologation due for March 1st, the Group A cars were taken into the hills behind San Remo for final fettling. There, in the hands of Lele Pinto and Mikki Biasion, they were put through their paces under the critical eye of Claudio Lombardi.

The latest car weighed in at 1150kgs with a full tank of fuel, much the same as its predecessor. Its more powerful engine, however, was 5kgs lighter at 153kgs. This new 2 litre developed a good 270bhp on the road and on the bench had been up to the 300bhp Group A limit. A new, vertically mounted intercooler lay beside the enlarged radiator and the T3 Garrett turbo was controlled in overboost by an electronic valve which limited pressure to a maximum of 1.4 atmospheres. The system of boost control was related through the electronics to engine speed, which ensured instant turbo response in all circumstances. Different camshafts opening larger valves were also evaluated on test, together with larger oil and water pumps.

The transmission, while fundamentally unchanged, used a ZF front differential and at the back a Ferguson system was tested alongside the usual Torsen. A new gearbox, with six forward speeds was available; the lightweight Kevlar propeller shaft of the HF4WD was retained and new, large diameter Brembo brakes were installed inside 9 x 16 speedline wheels. On test, everyone appeared satisfied. Biasion told Franco Nugnes, the reporter who witnessed the team at work, that it was 'more of a rally car than the 4WD, nervous but pleasing, secure and not spiteful.'

ABOVE **Victory in the American Olympus Rally gave Lancia the 1988 World Championship. It was, however, something of a hollow result for only 29 teams took part, none of them from major manufacturers. The Integrale was beginning to appear invincible.**

LEFT **The Acropolis Rally saw Lancias in the first four places, Biasion, Ericsson, Fiorio and Alen finishing in that order. The result put Biasion ahead in the '88 Drivers Championship.**

Perhaps it was only to be expected though that this satisfaction would not last. When the Integrale appeared for the first time in the World Championships in the Portuguese Rally, it was accompanied by extreme tension in the Lancia camp. Although Lancia had often won with a new car first time out – Stratos, S4 and HF4WD – no-one was complacent in Portugal. The Integrale might be no more than an extension of the 4WD, but it had much that was new and untried in competition about it. That this concern was justified was shown immediately the event began. Alen, on the first, preparatory Super special stage at Estoril had a differential fail, causing him to limp home some 12 minutes behind Biasion and down to 94th place before the rally had really began. Not unnaturally, he was furious. Being joint first in the Drivers Championship made him want 20 points from Portugal very much and here he was, let down by Lancia's newest car.

As if in anticipation of troubles of this kind, Lancia swamped the rally with cars. In addition to the four Martini Integrales entered for Alen, Biasion, Ericsson and Recalde, there were two HF4WD's for Fiorio and Loubet, a non-works Integrale for del Zoppo and private 4WD's for Caneva, Zanon, Nilsson and Bica. Of these eleven cars, five finished in the top ten places.

After his disastrous beginning, Alen, with a new transmission, quickly hauled himself back up the field. Although he had little chance of winning, it was not in his nature to concede and all place points were welcome. Biasion, of course, was in full flight, closely followed by Ericsson, Fiorio and Loubet, with Alen matching him in stage victories throughout the rally.

By the beginning of the third etape on the penultimate day, Biasion was comfortably in the lead. He left Pavoa nearly two minutes ahead of Auriol's Sierra Cosworth and by then it was clear that any possible Ford challenge had vanished. Not that all was well with Lancia. Ericsson's car had begun to show signs of transmission failure and eventually, on Stage 11, failed completely. Fiorio and Loubet, in their older cars, had no such problems. Routine shock absorber changes were all they needed. At one point Loubet lay second, just ahead of Fiorio but as the event progressed the young Italian

proved the faster. Alen, strong as ever after his initial set back, continued to advance but in the end only managed sixth place to Biasion's first, with Fiorio and Loubet second and third. It was no mean debut for the Integrale. Nor was the result anything but a source of pleasure for Fiorio senior and junior since Alex, with 30 points from two second places, now led the Drivers Championship by four points from Alen, Lancia's principal driver.

Yet the real test of the Integrale and the drivers was still to come. During their long rallying history

By the time Lancia went to the USA for the 1988 Olympus Rally the World Championship had been decided once again in their favour. In the world of rallying Lancia was then as dominant as McClaren and Porsche in other fields.

The Olympus Rally was sometimes as dusty as an Acropolis or the Safari. Here Biasion puts up a smoke screen on his way to a largely unopposed win. His team mate, Alex Fiorio, was second.

Lancia had won every major event but one. The missing link in this chain of success was the Safari, the great East African rally that had so often left the very best of professional teams floundering, or worse. Lancia had suffered with the rest but for 19 years, since three 1.3HF Fulvias took their first start in April 1969, the event had become something of an obsession. Certainly for Fiorio and his old number one, Sandro Munari, the Safari was the one event they longed to win. Over the years the cars had come close but could never manage better than second place. Now, in April 1988, it was the turn of the Integrale.

Much time and money was invested in preparation for the event. While Alen and Ericsson were up in Sweden in February, Biasion, Preston and a team of engineers and technicians were out in Kenya reconnoitring the whole route and setting up the Integrale for a win or bust attack on the Safari. As soon as he was able Alen joined them, but none of the drivers had an easy time. For one thing the new six speed gearbox, devised particularly with the Kenyan rally in mind, was far from trouble free. There were also high engine and tyre temperatures. Finally, the ever present question of the weather hung over all decisions, particularly since under dry conditions the heavier, more complex, four wheel drive cars had no advantage over simpler two wheel drive machines.

When it came to the rally itself, no-one could accuse Lancia of not trying. Although they reduced their planned entry of three cars down to two (Alen stayed home) in order to avoid stretching their support crews too far, their commitment was total. Biasion and Preston had both helicopter and fixed wing back-up, together with the most dedicated ground support. Their cars, carrying the usual, substantial roo bars and array of lights in front, were fitted with specially homologated six speed gearboxes and long travel suspension. As it turned out, the armour was necessary, for at one point Biasion hit a zebra at speed.

Despite this dramatic incident, Biasion won, giving Lancia the Safari victory they had sought so long. It did not come easily, though. The first sector, from Nairobi to Mombasa, saw Erwin Weber's Golf GTi leading Preston and Biasion. The second, which took the cars back to Nairobi, changed the order. Weber dropped back, Preston had his gearbox jam and Biasion lost time near Nairobi when his turbo failed. This put local driver Mike Kirkland, in a works Nissan 200SX, ahead.

The second leg, which ran north from the Kenyan capital, began badly. At Karatine, on the way to Nanyuki, cars were ambushed by rock barricades across the road. They were also stoned by spectators. Kirkland damaged his steering but Preston, who hit the rocks hard, had the transmission ripped out of his Integrale, damage which was quite beyond repair.

This left Biasion on his own. He hit his Zebra shortly after leaving Nanyuki, near Mt Kenya, and the damage was not fully repaired until he reached Eldoret. But later, after arriving at Nakuru, the Lancia crew made an almost fatal blunder. For some reason they forgot to hand in their time card, an error which usually led to disqualification. It was only the courtesy of Kirkland and the controller, Lord Delamere, which enabled the card to be retrieved and duly stamped. Without such sportsmanship Lancia's rally would have ended there and then.

With such good fortune on their side it would have indeed been bitter had Biasion and Siviero not then won. Lancia, recognising this and seeing the Safari at last within their reach, played safe from then on. With their shepherding helicopters front and rear, Biasion and Siviero set off on the final leg, determined to win. Even then, much of the final distance was done with a damaged shock absorber, though not so slowly as to lose time. In the end the Integrale team won by 12 minutes from Kirkland and the big Nissan. Lancia's joy was boundless.

By now they were virtually out of sight at the head of the World Championship, having won all of the first four events. Biasion, with his 20 Kenyan points, led the Drivers Championship and the next event, the Tour de Corse, could also have been expected to go their way. To the relief of everyone outside Turin it did not.

Unlike the Safari, which Lancia had never previously won, the Tour de Corse was high on their list of expected successes. Virtually a mountain road race, the circuitous Corsican stages suited Italian cars and drivers. Accordingly, Lancia, despite previous tragedies, regarded the island rally as a sure source of points and it was through no fault of the two French members of the team, Loubet and Saby, that Lancia had to be content with second and third places. Although he won 22 of the 30 special stages, Loubet was ultimately forced to concede victory to Didier Auriol's Sierra Cosworth, a concession forced on him by a failed gearbox. Unable to retrieve the time lost as a consequence, the newest recruit to the Lancia squad had to give best to the Cosworth, which achieved Ford's first ever Corsican victory.

As if to emphasise their surprise at being beaten in Corsica, the team immediately proceeded to take the first four places in the Acropolis Rally, which followed in late May. The order was Biasion, Ericsson, Fiorio and Alen, which put Biasion ahead in the Drivers Championship. At the beginning of the season Fiorio had announced that there would be no finishing orders imposed upon the team during the year, nor would the 1987 seven start agreement hold. 'They can fight it out among themselves', he said, obviously irritated by the criticism of his control of the previous season's results. But by mid season this had been forgotten. In Greece, once it became clear that Lancia drivers had seen off the opposition, instructions went out to hold position. Biasion was ahead at the time.

It is always tempting to be critical of anything that smacks of arrangement in sporting matters. This is perhaps too simplistic a view when the sport is as complex and costly as world class rallying. Lancia, and other teams, have always to gain the maximum benefit from their investment and this certainly means winning as much as possible. In the 1988 season, with the Integrale totally dominating the Championship, could Fiorio have been expected to do anything other than support one of his Italian drivers in pursuit of the Drivers Championship? Since the success of the Group A Deltas, Lancia's market share had soared, especially in Italy, where the company was second only to Fiat in volume of cars sold. An Italian World Champion would promote the marque even more.

The Acropolis result virtually confirmed Lancia as World Champions. If they were to win the next event, the Olympus in the USA, they could not be overtaken and they would be Champions by June. They did and they were. Biasion won and Alex Fiorio was second, in a poorly supported rally with only 29 starters. No major team other than Lancia bothered to go to America: it seemed as if they had all thrown in the towel, unable to cope with the dominance of the Integrale.

And yet, and yet: in the background, glimpsed

Following his success in a privately entered but works backed Delta in the previous year's New Zealand Rally, Franz Wittman was given a works drive in Argentina in 1988. As always, spectacular water splashes attract photographers.

and then forgotten, were signs of change. Toyota, new to the World Championship in 1987 and now beginning to take matters seriously, sent their latest Celica GT-Four Group A cars to Greece for Kankkunen and Waldegaard to drive. Until the Toyota's transmissions failed, both put pressure on the Lancias. At one stage Kankkunen, no doubt to his quiet pleasure, led the rally and Fiorio senior was unable to order the result until his Toyota retired.

Lancia sensed that the new Japanese challenge might well prove more significant than Mazda's had been. In Finland's Thousand Lakes, Kank-

kunen's Celica had matched Alen's Integrale for speed and adhesion, only finally failing on Stage 33 when the engine exploded. Alen and Ericsson went on to take first and second places for Lancia, but back at Abarth, Lombardi and his engineers paid even more attention to extracting the most from the Integrale for the coming year. The season, however, was theirs and as it progressed the predictable accumulation of victories continued. Everything Lancia's Integrale entered it won; Argentina, The Thousand Lakes, San Marino and the Lombard RAC all went Lancia's way. They started every one of the 11 World Championship rallies and won ten, dropping points only in Corsica. They amassed 217 points from a possible total of 220. Never before had a manufacturer so totally dominated the Championship. In rallying, Lancia assumed a similar role to Porsche in the world of

Alen at the crossroads. The Finnish driver won his first RAC Rally at the end of the 1988 season. This was one of the few events that had previously eluded him and his victory also gave him the greatest number of firsts achieved by any rally driver in international competition.

sports car racing. Stopping them would be a major problem for their competitors.

Their drivers, inevitably, were also dominant. The 1988 World Championship for Drivers was virtually restricted to those who drove works Integrales. Initially either Biasion, Alen or Fiorio was capable of coming out on top but as time passed everything pointed towards the prize going Biasion's way. Up to mid summer Fiorio and Alen stayed close enough to challenge his leading position but after Argentina, where he was beaten into second place by Lancia's local guest driver, Jorge Recalde, the Championship was almost his. San Remo clinched it. Neither Toyota nor Ford offered any sustained challenge to a Lancia team that took the first four places, Biasion, Fiorio, Cerrato and Alen finishing line astern. Lancia had pulled off yet another double, one made the more sweet by being entirely home grown. Italian chests swelled.

One other trophy remained. Markku Alen, Lancia's long suffering senior driver, finally won the RAC. After many years of trying, driving everything from an Escort to a Stratos, he made it in the Integrale. It was also his 19th World Championship victory, the greatest number achieved by any driver, ever.

9 *A car for all seasons*

NOTHING IS QUITE so encouraging as success. With company fortunes revived by two consecutive World Rally Championships, Lancia sales grew apace and with them that innovative research and development which had long been a company hallmark. Fiat's investment and the high level of engineering skill at Abarth and at Lancia headquarters in Turin's via Vincenzo Lancia, combined to give them a central role in research for the whole group. With big money behind them Lancia's engineers experimented freely and most productively.

In the domain of the Delta, certain important developments occurred. Elsewhere within Fiat, other research produced results which, while not immediately useful, had longer term significance for the Group A Integrale or, as was most likely, its heir. Of this work, the prototype Group S rally cars, the ECV1 and ECV2 were the most glamorous; the most utilitarian was the development of four wheel steering and the work of greatest use to the rally team was a new 16 valve engine and the Valeo electronic clutch.

The ECV1 was first shown publicly in 1986 at the Bologna Motor Show. It was an utterly radical, mid-engined, total traction machine, bearing some external resemblance to the S4 but in fact derived from the Fiat VSS (Vettura Sperimentale a Sottosistemi) of 1981. Fiat's original work had been concerned largely with the use of plastics in non-load bearing parts of the car but Lancia, when they took over the project, moved on to study the role of composite materials throughout the vehicle. Responsibility for the research lay with Claudio Lombardi who, in an interview with the prestigious Italian magazine, *Quattroruote* in September 1988, explained its importance to Lancia. 'The starting point for this research was Lancia's commitment to the World Rally Championship. The first studies and the prototype of 1985 were intended to improve the performance of the S4. When the changed regulations of 1986 excluded Group B cars, we went on to make use of our experience by producing a mobile laboratory with which we could master the uses of composites like carbon fibre, kevlar and so on and also improve the efficiency of our 4 cylinder forced induction engines.'

When asked about the advances made by the ECV over the S4, Lombardi continued: 'As far as the chassis is concerned, the S4 was built up from a trellis of rigid steel tubes, capable of easy repair when damaged and giving easy access to mechanical components. The new materials are not so good in this respect but have the big advantage of allowing a very stiff monocoque to be built that is 20% lighter. But this is not the end of the story. The work is of great interest to companies wishing to produce limited edition sports cars in numbers under 1000 annually. Composite materials, apart from working well, don't cost much to produce and there is little expensive tooling required. Mechanically, the new "Triflux" engine uses twin turbos. It is an in-line four able to run at lower cylinder head temperatures and less inclined to distort and damage gaskets.'

The 'Triflux' cylinder head described by Lombardi was significant. Working with his colleague Giovanni Roffina, Lombardi developed an earlier concept, known as F.I.D. (Flusso invertito doppie) into a four valve system in which the inlets lay in a single line down the centre of the head with the exhaust valves on each side. This allowed for three gas flows – hence 'Triflux'- which brought with

The ECV engine, with its clever 'Triflux' head was able to produce over 600 bhp from a mere 1759cc. This Lombardi designed engine derived from earlier work undertaken by Fiat researchers, and had it ever gone into production for competition use, Group B rallying would have become the most demanding and risky form of motor sport yet devised.

ABOVE **While ECV developments were dramatic and radical, the road cars evolved through a series of smaller increments, mostly concerned with traction, stability and driver confidence. Integrale promotion emphasised these points.**

them twin exhaust channels, twin turbos and an equal distribution of heat along each side of the head. The central inlet tract remained correspondingly cooler than with a conventional layout.

This 1759cc engine produced 600bhp at 8000rpm and developed 55kgm of torque at 5000rpm. It drove a mean machine, whose all up weight was a mere 910kgs, about the same as a Ful-

RIGHT **ECV1 (top) bore some distant, visual relationship to the road going Deltas and Integrales (bottom) but was actually a direct descendant of the S4. As an engineering test bed it has significance for today's cars.**

via 1.6 Lusso. If the S4 had been as ferocious as its drivers claimed – and Fiorio felt no-one was capable of concentrating fully on its wicked nature all of the time – what on earth would the ECV, once introduced into Group S rallying, have been like?

The form it may well have taken was expressed by its re-embodiment, ECV2. If ECV1 drew on the S4, ECV2 was a beautiful advance on both. Like

the first car, whose chassis and running gear it used, ECV2 was a mid-engined coupe intended solely for competition. It was powerful, purposeful and compact. Although its 2440cm wheelbase was the same as the S4, it was longer than the Stratos (which, at 2180cm was about the size of a Fiat 850) but noticeably smaller than the Integrale in all dimensions.

Both versions of the ECV used a monocoque body made of carbon fibre material, impregnated with epoxy resins and formed into composite sheets with a honeycomb core. The second derivative, however, was given a far more aerodynamic shape in which great care had been taken to control pressure zones. This was particularly noticeable in the front, where areas of high pressure enabled greater volumes of cooling air to be introduced. Lombardi described the evolution of the ECV2 thus: 'While retaining the chassis and mechanical

The plastic monocoque of the ECV2 was designed and wind tunnel tested to produce adequate airflow at low speeds, providing reliable engine cooling under the widely differing conditions of international rallying.

characteristics of the first prototype we have improved the airflow and temperature control, enabling us to put the water and oil radiators at the front and to reduce the space they occupy. We have also developed smaller, water cooled intercoolers for the turbos with the overall effect of allowing us to design a clean, compact, aerodynamically efficient body. Of course, in rally cars, high top speed is not important. What is needed is a body that contributes to maximum adhesion and provides effective cooling at lower speeds. It is also important to distribute the masses as equally as possible between front and rear, concentrating them around

The high wing and radically formed tail of the ECV2 offered control at speed in what was an essentially unstable and consequently extremely nimble rally car. "Clean, compact, aerodynamically efficient" In Lombardi's words.

the centre of the car to give a low polar moment. In doing just this we have produced an ideal, manageable rally car.'

Engine design also evolved with the ECV2. Capacity increased to 1.8 litres and the twin turbochargers were reconfigured into what was described as a 'modular' form. This meant that instead of running continuously, each turbo was separately controlled through an electronic valve. At low engine speeds only one was used, but as revolutions increased the second turbo came in gradually, giving smooth, lag free acceleration. On test at La Mandria the car did all that was required of it.

What it was never to do, of course, was run in anger under Lancia Martini colours. That task still fell to the Integrale which, for the 1989 season, was to be given a new 16 valve engine rated at 195 bhp. Plans were also in hand to provide faster, more efficient and less breakable gear changes through a novel electronic clutch. This two pedal system was devised and developed by the Italian company Valeo, working closely with Abarth and particularly with Felice Garrone and Enrico Alviano, Lombardi's gearbox and electronics experts. It was an essentially simple and elegant concept. A dry, two plate clutch, operated electromechanically, received its instructions from an electronic controller. Lombardi described this as the robot. It was programmed by the driver through a dashboard control and could be set to take up appropriately on asphalt, loose gravel or snowy surfaces, or set for normal road use. Additionally there was a manual button on the steering wheel rim enabling the driver to over-ride the automatic control. This was essential for racing starts.

The central controller received data from the gear lever, the throttle, the gear selectors, the first motion shaft and an engine speed sensor. Operation was simple. When the gear lever was moved, the clutch disengaged. As soon as the next gear was selected and the engine speed was appropriate, it re-engaged. Engagement did not occur automatically below 1200rpm.

Drivers liked the clutch on test. Biasion and Lele Pinto used it a lot, finding it particularly good in snow. In all circumstances the electronic system gave quicker changes than those achieved with conventional controls and, as a result, plans were made for it to be homologated in time for use on the 1989 Monte.

The new season brought with it the prospect of serious challenges to Lancia's dominant position. Not only Toyota were in contention but also Mazda and newcomers Mitsubishi posed a threat which, if not fully realised immediately, was certainly growing apace. In preparing to cope with this, Fiorio pulled off something of a coup in signing the outstanding French driver, Didier Auriol, to replace Kankkunen, who had moved to Toyota. Auriol, who had been actively pursued by Toyota and by Ford, with whom he drove in 1987 and 1988, was brought in as an asphalt specialist. He also had considerable gravel skills which, in association with the all round abilities of Alen and Biasion, his new Lancia colleagues, could be expected to get the most out of the latest Integrales.

Lancia also took the unusual step of contracting a driver to specially prepare for the Safari. Jorge Recalde was sent out to East Africa in December to work with a team of engineers in getting cars ready for Spring, when Lancia planned to defend their 1988 Kenyan victory by sending three cars to be driven by Biasion, Alen and Recalde.

As had happened so often in the past, Lancia's homologation plans for the 1989 season went astray. The 16 valve engine was not ready for Monte Carlo and the team's first outing was made with the old 8 valve cars. Unusually, however, for the first time the season did not begin in Monaco but was launched with the Swedish Rally, now removed by FISA from the World Championship for Rallies, the manufacturers' event, and only eligible for the Drivers Championship. As a result of FISA's insistence that it be run in early January, the event was poorly supported by factory teams, for whom Monte Carlo preparation took precedence.

Lancia was among the abstentions. Nevertheless, private and semi works Integrales did appear and those of Per Eklund and Mikael Ericsson finished second and fourth respectively.

Of those Integrales starting the Monte, when it came, five were works cars. The three Martini Lancias, driven by Biasion, Auriol and Bruno Saby, wore new liveries and all had standard, three pedal controls. Valeo's electronic clutch, although effective, was not considered wholly reliable and was only fitted to Alex Fiorio's Group A Jolly Club car. The second Jolly, driven by Darrio Cerrato accompanied by Italian TV reporter Gianni Vasino, had conventional controls. Cerrato, driving the event without pace notes and saddled with an amateur navigator, had enough to cope with without an experimental clutch adding to his burden.

It was a successful but tragic event, marked by total victory for the works team and a shocking, fatal accident caused by Alex Fiorio's car leaving the road on Stage 5 and crashing downhill into spectators, among whom was the Swedish rally driver Lars Eric Torph and his navigator Bertil Rehnfeldt. Torph was killed immediately and Rehnfeldt died later.

Why the car crashed is uncertain. On the stage there was considerable crowd indiscipline, but the accident happened on an undemanding section. Some attempt was made to blame the two pedal controls of the car but with no justification. Whatever the reason, the accident cast a blight on a rally otherwise characterised by a spirited, unrestricted battle between Biasion and Auriol for first place and an early, though brief, challenge from Kankkunen's Toyota. In the end Biasion won, followed by Auriol and Saby, with Mikkola's Mazda in fourth place.

Monotony was setting in again. When the finishing order was repeated a month later in Portugal, the longed for challenge from such as Toyota seemed a chimera. For pundits and public alike the Biasion, Alen, Fiorio result was yet another whitewash, the more so since six of the first ten finishers drove Integrales and one, Carlo Bica, finished sixth in an older HF4WD.

Yet the rally had been far from trouble-free. The final result belied the pressure applied to Biasion by Carlo Sainz, Toyota's up and coming Spanish driver. At halfway he was second, within two minutes of the leading Lancia and had he not hit a tree at the beginning of Stage 16, who knows what damage he might have done to Lancia's self-esteem. The Italians had also to contend with their fair share of mechanical troubles. Alen was often

Lancia's victory in the 1989 Monte Carlo Rally was
achieved with the previous season's 8 valve
Integrale, the new 16 valve engine not having been
homologated.

ABOVE **Jorge Recalde, seen here, was outpaced by Biasion in the '89 Safari. The Italian driver drove consistently throughout the event to give Lancia victory for the second year running.**

BELOW **They were less successful the following year. Only Kankkunen's car survived, no doubt because of Lancia's redoubtable service team and the Finnish driver's steady determination.**

brakeless and sometimes in differential difficulties. Fiorio had trouble with his two pedal car and quickly reverted to three. Auriol went out on Stage 29 with clutch failure, leaving only Biasion to storm through Portugal unblemished.

So far it was all a rerun of 1988. Lancia led the World Championship for Rallies with maximum points and Biasion was top of the drivers league. The Safari, which followed on March 23rd, maintained the pattern. Biasion won again from Mike Kirkland in the Nissan 200SX. Recalde, he of the long reconnaissance, had a great drive until he hit a goat. Alex Fiorio, who appeared instead of the expected Alen, finished 10th. Fiorio's performance was the more creditable in that his Jolly Club car doubled as a chase car, complete with spare parts

Auriol achieved an excellent second place to Biasion in Portugal in 1990. Works Integrales, now in 300bhp 16 valve form, swept the board, despite the departure of the long serving Alen in the direction of Subaru.

and a team mechanic as co-driver!

The pleasure of a second Safari victory, great as it was for all concerned, was particularly keen for one man. Claudio Lombardi, the technical inspiration behind all of Lancia's recent World Championship cars, unexpectedly found himself projected forward into the hot seat as Competition Director for Lancia in place of the redoubtable Cesare Fiorio. Fiorio, whose skills in team management were legendary, had been quite suddenly despatched to Maranello to take charge of Ferrari's Formula One team. His rapid departure, after nearly 30 years continuous commitment to Lancia, left a gap only Lombardi could fill and his first task had been to oversee the team's Safari efforts.

What other consequences would follow from Fiorio's precipitate translation from Turin to Modena and from rallying to the sniping squabbles of Ferrari, were hard to predict. Lombardi was a brilliant engineer but whether he had the political temperament for team management remained to be seen. Certainly, other changes would occur and

ABOVE **Italy 1989; Auriol's Integrale wears the short lived, strident red livery that marked Lancia's brief return to the Italian national Grand Prix colour.**

BELOW **Bruno Saby, by way of contrast, turned out for the Tour de Corse in Lancia Blue and white, a colour scheme reminiscent of Gianni Lancia's works B20 GT coupés of the early 1950's.**

Rain ensured that the all-French team held off the challenge from the BMW M3's and the Sierra Cosworths in the Tour de Corse.

one such was the return of Giorgio Pianta to Lancia from his sojourn with Alfa.

Meanwhile the schedule continued.

The Tour de Corse, when it came, marked the end of a run of failures in the French event. Not since 1984, when Alen drove an 037, had Lancia taken 20 points in the island road race. Now, aided by the weather, Auriol repeated his 1988 victory, but this time in the Integrale. Following past practice, Lombardi ran a wholly French team comprising Auriol, Loubet and Saby, who drove a French-sponsored car. Although initially dry conditions favoured the BMW M3's and Sierra Cosworths, with the arrival of the rain events swung sharply in Lancia's favour.

Throughout the rally Auriol's closest competitor was Francois Chatriot in a Pro Drive BMW. In fact the BMW driver took more special stages than Auriol but in the final analysis it was the Italian car that won by 2 minutes.

The next victory, in the Acropolis, gave Lancia

ABOVE **Biasion's win in the '89 Acropolis Rally gave Lancia the Grand Slam – ten consecutive victories in ten consecutive starts. No other car in rallying history had proved as successful as the Delta and Lancia gained enormous benefit from the Indian Summer of what was really an outdated design.**

RIGHT **From right to left – Biasion, Lombardi and Siviero take a bow following their Acropolis victory.**

the Grand Slam – ten consecutive wins in ten consecutive starts. However, this was only part of a growing and remarkable achievement. Since the Acropolis of 1987 the Delta HF4WD and its successor, the Integrale, had won every rally started, with the exception of the 1988 Tour de Corse. This meant 21 victories out of a possible 22. No other rally car had such a record: not the Mini, not the Fulvia, not the Alpine, Stratos, 131, Escort RS,

Driver Ericsson, left and navigator Bilstam, right. Although Lancia always had Italian drivers in the team they were astute enough to ensure that they also included at least one Finn.

Quattro, Peugeot 205 nor any of the fine machines that grabbed the limelight for a season or two before being consumed by the next star. Only the Delta, plucked from near retirement and rejuvenated remarkably, achieved such total dominance.

Reasons were not hard to find. Lancia took rallying seriously. They had been in the first rank for twenty five years and had prepared cars for every sort of motor sport throughout the whole of their history. Good Lancias had style, were discreet, often arrived first, were without flash but glittered, none the less. And inside they were well engineered. Engineering derived from competition made the Integrale what it was. It succeeded in Group A because Lancia, more than any of their competitors, could translate the technologies of their S4 racer directly into a road car and then back again into the new rules World Championship. As the emphasis swung towards total traction, Lancia won because it had the best system. The HF4WD was not the most powerful rally car in the begin-

ning, but it conducted itself better. After again giving New Zealand a miss, the team's next appointment was in Argentina. Given that Lancia now led the Championship by 100 points to Toyota's 36, a poor works entry in the South American event was only to be expected. None of the other factories was willing to spend the considerable sums involved in flying cars and crews to the bottom of the world for no good reason. With only local competition to contend with, Lancia took the first three places and won every special stage. The upset came with the final order. Jorge Recalde, expected to win, finished third; Mikael Ericsson, too often Lancia's fall guy, won and won convincingly from Alex Fiorio. Such an unanticipated result did much for Ericsson's self confidence for, with 30 points, he now lay fourth in the Drivers Championship, 10 points behind Fiorio.

Such proximity may have cost him his promised drive in Australia in mid September. Lancia, having clinched the World Championship for Rallies with their Argentinian win, now had to look to the Drivers Championship. Biasion still led by 36 points but Ericsson, who won the 100 Lakes on his return from Argentina (but not in a Lancia), had closed up to joint second with Didier Auriol.

The Finnish result marked the beginning of the end for the 8 valve Integrale. Martini Lancia sent Biasion, Alen and Auriol to represent them. Every effort had been made to provide them with new 16 valve cars for the event but once again the company failed to meet the homologation target. With insuf-ficient power available to them, the Lancia drivers found themselves in the unfamiliar position of also-rans. Finland and the Japanese had finally knocked the Integrale on the head.

That the principal blow was delivered by their reserve driver wearing other colours added insult to injury. Ericsson, denied a Lancia drive on his own ground, was released to Mitsubishi for the event. Doubtless the powers that be in the Corso Marche had not felt threatened by such a combination and their chagrin at the result of their magnanimity can only be imagined.

Australia saw them routed again, this time by the Toyota GT Fours of Kankkunen and Kenneth Eriksson. Alen managed to hold on to third place but it was clear to everyone that the 8 valve Integrale had had its day.

10 Finale

ANOTHER NEW LIVERY, 16 valves, 290 official bhp, 41kgm of torque at 4500rpm and six forward gears put Lancia back on top. Never mind the Japanese challenge; at San Remo the regenerated Integrale shut the lid on it – but only just.

Martini Lancia's victory over the Toyota of Carlos Sainz was as narrow as could be for Biasion and second place man Fiorio, a mere 15 seconds separating first and third. In fact, only a last minute throttle fault pulled the Toyota driver down. Up to then he had held firmly on to a lead taken from Fiorio on the last of the Tuscan stages behind Mercatello, only dropping back on Stage 29 as the rally neared its end.

For the first time since the days of Squadra Corse HF and Marlboro sponsorship, Lancias were again running in red, a new, jazzy, Martini colour scheme stridently announcing this newest, most powerful Integrale in broken Martini stripes as complex in arrangement as its underbonnet technology.

When the 16v car hit the streets for the first time it was greeted with applause. Behind it, growing sales figures indicated the enthusiasm generated by its predecessors, for since the introduction of the HF4WD, over 15000 total traction Deltas had been sold. Of these, 5298 were HF4WD cars and between 1987 and '89 a further 9841 Integrales were bought. Such figures gave great encouragement to Lancia's management and when the 16 valve car went on to achieve sales of 12486 and 20% of the European 4X4 market in the years 1989 and 1990, the investment in rallying looked more sound than ever. And of course it was not only these most glamorous Deltas that benefited. The less dramatic models sold in vastly greater numbers on the strength of their sporting sister's success and

Lancia's total sales in Italy were second only to those of Fiat by the time the 1980's came to a close.

But capping the sophistication of the 8 valve Integrale was not merely a matter of squeezing another 8 valves into a new head. The 16 valve head certainly helped the engine to produce more power (bringing the new road car's output close to that of the original Group A HF4WD and giving it nearly as much torque at 30.4kgm at 3000rpm) but of itself was only part of the story. The introduction of a greater number of smaller valves brought with it a smaller diameter Garrett T3 turbocharger, water cooled and able to accelerate more rapidly at lower engine speeds. A revised Weber-Marelli IAW engine management system also evolved, allowing, among other things, for the use of lead free petrol: it also offered more precisely controlled overboost by monitoring air temperatures, engine speed and throttle position.

The increased power of the road car, now up to 196CV at 5500rpm, was transmitted through a new hydraulic clutch and a ZF gearbox derived from the Ferrari-engined Thema 8.32. The transmission remained unchanged in design but acquired a new torque split, power now being divided in a proportion of 47/53 per cent. This was a direct consequence of rally experience, for the Integrale had always proved something of an under steerer at the limit. By sending more power to the rear wheels this tendency was counteracted (though not eliminated it should be said). Brakes were also improved, as was the suspension, damping and rubber. 105/50R Michelin MXX tyres mounted on 7x15" wheels were carried on tougher lower wishbones and shorter, stiffer coil springs. A new, stout anti-roll bar was fitted in front.

Companies go rallying for promotional reasons. Consequently, the ability to handle the media is an important quality in a manager and Fiorio excelled in this as he did in every other aspect of international rallying.

As an optional extra a clever ABS system, developed jointly with Bosch, became available. Fitting anti-lock brakes to so sophisticated a drive system as the Integrale's was not easy. The braking system could become confused by the action of a particular wheel under the control of its limited slip differential and on mixed surfaces a conflict between the brake sensors and the drive control would not be reassuring. Bosch and Lancia therefore devised a controller capable of responding to lateral and longitudinal loads in addition to normal brake inputs. This dealt most effectively with the full range of signals generated by cornering and differential wheel grip.

All of these advances were packaged into a low, tough looking car, much like its predecessor but distinguished by a manifest power bulge on the bonnet and rather flash trim. It went like stink and everyone who drove it said it was wonderful; yes, wonderful but not of course perfect.

British road testers were generally less critical than Italian. The racing driver Ivan Capelli, writing in *Quattroruote*, felt that the car was more useable on the track than on the road, largely because of an absence of response at low speed. Above 4000rpm the motor was fine but this led to a lot of gear changing to keep it on song. On the other hand, its circuit potential was marred by final understeer. He was also a little critical of steering response and of brake fade. What he liked, however, was what everyone seemed to like – the car's stability, security, stunning high speed performance once the turbo was fully committed and the reassuring competence of the ABS braking system. Throughout Europe the general opinion of motoring writers seemed to be that even if the car was not perfect, it was the best there was.

The Group A Martini Lancias did not appear again in 1989. Since the team was already World Champion and Biasion had retained his World Drivers crown, why risk their reputations unnecessarily? There was still much to do to the 16v Integrale and time was precious. Nevertheless, a 16 valve Group N car, entered by Top Run

ABOVE **October 1990 saw Kankkunen finish second to Auriol in the San Remo Rally. The event gave Lancia the World Championship yet again but notice of intent was given by Carlos Sainz, who won the Drivers Championship in his Toyota.**

BELOW **Daniel Cerrato's Fina Integrale on a coast road during the San Remo event.**

Racing, did appear in the Ivory Coast Rally, only to retire early on. Two other Top Run Integrales. both 8 valve Group N machines, also failed, one after determinedly leading the rally for some time before it went out with a broken cam belt.

Sadly, Lancia blotted their copy book at the end of the season with their last minute withdrawal from the Lombard RAC in November. This did not go unnoticed and Ericsson and Alen, who had been scheduled to drive in Britain, were particularly annoyed. Even though both were leaving the team, each would have relished the opportunity to score a final 20 points for Lancia and, from a distance, it seemed as if they were perhaps being reprimanded.

Alen, particularly, would have been justified in feeling let down. After 16 years of loyal service to the Turin empire, during which time he delivered 18 World Championship 1st places to either Fiat or Lancia, he might have expected the opportunity to have at least sought another team for the RAC. Yet such was the timing of Lancia's belated withdrawal, this was impossible for him. Ericsson, due to drive for Toyota in 1990, was left similarly high and dry.

With two of their drivers moving to Japanese teams – Alen had signed for Subaru – Lancia's 1990 line up comprised Biasion, Auriol and Juha Kankkunen. Kankkunen's return to the Integrale was something of a surprise, since his 1987 Lancia season had not always been happy. Despite this he obviously felt that he would achieve more with the Turin team than with Toyota, where he had spent the 1988 and 1989 seasons. Supporting the three front line Martini Lancia drivers were Daniel Cerrato in Jolly Club colours and Alex Fiorio wearing either, as necessary. Also available were Yves Loubet and, in a French Lancia Fina Integrale, Bruno Saby. It was a pretty powerful array.

Monte Carlo once again assumed its place as the first rally of the season, the previous year's aberrant decision to begin in Sweden having been forgotten. It was a rally of anniversaries and scandal, with Lancia once more in the thick of it, as had so often

The Thousand Lakes Rally in 1990 was a sorry affair for the Lancia team. The Japanese trounced them and Kankkunen, their highest placed finisher, could manage no better than fifth.

Lancia's 1990 Safari saw a reversion to the troubles of earlier years. All of the Integrale 8 valve cars suffered from overheating and other mechanical problems and Biasion, shown here, eventually retired with a broken con-rod. But Kankkunen held out for second place.

happened in previous Monte's. For the first time in years the rally was wholly centred upon Monaco itself. Recent past practice of dispersing the start of the competitive section to towns in France was dropped in recognition, particularly, of the Centenary of the Automobile Club de Monaco. Monegasque hoteliers and competitors alike welcomed this reversion.

With Toyota, Mazda and Mitsubishi all strongly represented, Lancia knew that real pressure was to be expected, not just in the prestigious Monte but throughout the coming season. Toyota particularly intended to break their dominance and the Celica GT Fours of Carlo Sainz, Mikael Ericsson and Armin Schwarz were backed with formidable technical resources. Lombardi and his men accordingly pulled out all the stops and the 16 valve Integrales entered the lists in as potent a form as possible.

Various innovations, including a new 'direct static' ignition system which used a small coil on each spark plug raised power to 295 bhp. Larger water and oil radiators were fitted and a gearbox oil cooler was also available. The transmission was beefed up all round and the Kevlar propeller shaft given special attention to enable it to cope with the extra torque of the new engine. The Brembo brakes were given larger 332mm front discs and on some events Kevlar/fibreglass cooling 'fans' were worn on the outer wheel surfaces.

Thus equipped, Martini Lancia's drivers set out

Biasion on Safari once again. His team mate Alex Fiorio also retired with a siezed engine, leaving Kankkunen to hang on to the end to defend second place.

Memory of better days. '89 Safari winner Biasion sprays champagne. The following year was to be less successful.

on the 58th Monte Carlo Rally, the 200th in the World series and the start of their 25th year as a works team. Cesare Fiorio's HF Squadra Corse, begun in 1963, had been taken over formally by Lancia in 1965, since when no other team had been so determinedly and consistently successful. The present generation of drivers inevitably had much expected of them.

The rally, when it came, was fast and eventful. Without snow, as a result of the exceptionally mild winter, the Monegasque event became more like the Tour de Corse. Slicks were much in evidence

and driving techniques required modification. In a rally characterised by mechanical failures – Saby had ignition and brake troubles, Cerato's turbo failed and Biasion smashed his windscreen on stage six and later developed electronic hiccups – Auriol and Sainz quickly became the front runners.

Following their Safari defeat Lancia took heart from Auriol's win in the next event, the Tour de Corse. This time the Frenchman turned the tables on Toyota by beating Sainz into second place, overcoming various mechanical troubles.

Behind them, as they swapped the lead in the closest of close contests, accidents occurred. The French Renault driver, Jean-Claude Bertaudier, was killed above Burzet; a spectator was injured on the Privas stage, leading to its cancellation; and Kankkunen, new to the 16v car's performance, crashed out of the event on Stage 4.

Auriol and Sainz were never challenged. As the end came in sight the Toyota driver seemed to have the edge. Dramatically, however, Auriol suddenly brought the Integrale to the front, slicing the Toyota's times over the last stages in such a way as to create disbelief among his rivals. The advantage built by Sainz on the first round of the Final (Stages 20-28) was demolished by the Lancia driver, who went on to win by nearly 1 minute.

But the victory did not go uncontested. Rumour had it that the winning Integrale was not what it seemed and Toyota lodged a protest, claiming that Lancia had used an improperly sealed turbo. What

they were really suggesting was that the mandatory 40mm restriction, required by FISA regulations, had been tampered with. This, they believed, was the source of Auriol's remarkable turn of speed in the closing stages. Despite some circumstantial evidence the protest was rejected by the stewards and Lancia were awarded their final place, a result wholly earned by Auriol's inspired endgame, made possible by a 'go faster' chip installed to raise turbo pressures for the final charge. A later appeal to the FIA was also dismissed.

February came and went without the customary trip to Sweden. No snow in the north made the rally pointless and it was cancelled. That meant Portugal next stop. Here, in early March, Lancia swept the board. After initial challenges from Mitsubishi, Mazda and Toyota were disposed of, the Integrales came home line astern – Biasion, Auriol, Kankkunen, Cerrato and Bica finishing one to five. Recalde came seventh in an 8 valve car and Ronald Holzer brought a Lancia Deutschland Integrale into tenth place.

The unnatural weather of northern Europe that had so distorted the early rounds of the season extended to Africa in 1990. After several years absence from the Safari, the rainy season which had so often turned the rally into a mud bath, established itself early. Rivers rose, mudholes appeared and the pattern of the rally reverted to the old struggle with the weather that made the Safari unique. Lancia had never previously done well in the wet but, having won on the last two occasions, went to Africa hoping for a hat trick. As usual, they spent

Kankkunen's second place in the Acropolis kept the points coming, though by now Lancia realised that they no longer had everything their own way.

much time from January onward in preparation and their team of Biasion, Fiorio and Kankkunen arrived in Nairobi for the start on April 11th in optimistic mood.

A perennial problem for all Safari cars was engine temperature. Keeping things cool preoccupied drivers and engineers alike. The Integrale, with so much stuff packed under the bonnet, needed a lot of cooling, particularly in 16 valve form. The team therefore chose to use 8 valve engines for the event.

Principal competition came from Toyota and from the new Subaru team, which comprised six cars and included Markku Alen, late of Lancia, as team leader. As soon as the rally started, Lombardi must have regretted losing the Finn. Although his Legacy 4WD Turbo was an older, five speed model and not the new 6 speeder being prepared by Prodrive in England, Alen went into an immediate lead. That the car failed down in the Taita Hills, near Voi, was no reflection on either Alen or Subaru. The demanding conditions under which the rally was run knocked out half of all starters by the

LEFT **Auriol, exhaust flaming, heads for a Finnish lake and no points in a Thousand Lakes rally that was a disaster for Lancia. Kankkunen held onto fifth place.**

ABOVE **Historic array outside the York Motor Museum prior to the 1990 Australian Rally sees the Delta lined up beside the Stratos, one of its great predecessors in rallying history.**

end of that first etape. Mud was the major problem.

Nothing went really well for Lancia. Although Biasion moved to the front briefly during the fourth etape, Waldegaard, making a one-off drive for Toyota, soon regained the lead he had established early on. Later, on Stage 61, near Eldoret, Biasion finally dropped out with a smashed con-rod, joining Fiorio on the sidelines. Alessandro's engine had seized on stage 39.

With the two Italians out of the event it was left to Kankkunen to salvage something from the Safari. Although Lancia sat on top of the Championship table, Toyota were pressing hard and points were needed. Clearly, barring the unexpected, Walde-gaard would give the Japanese top marks in Africa but Lancia hoped for something from the rally, preferably 17 points. Kankkunen, driving dependably and with great resolution did not disappoint. He stayed close to Waldegaard all the way to achieve a good second place, 17 points which also did much for his own morale.

The next event, the Tour de Corse, reversed the finishing order. Didier Auriol won from Carlos Sainz and Lancia led the Championship by 23 points. Sainz, however, was closing on Auriol in the Drivers Championship, the Lancia driver having a mere 15 points advantage. For Auriol the Corsican victory was his third in a row. Supported by French team mate Yves Loubet, who retired on Stage 17, Auriol stayed ahead of Sainz and the Toyota to win by 36 seconds, though his rally was far from un-eventful. During its course both Integrales suffered from transmission troubles. Loubet broke half shafts and Auriol, a mere three stages from the fin-ish, had a major transmission failure which almost put him out of the rally. Only the competence of the Martini Lancia mechanics saved the day and gave Lancia the full 20 points they sorely needed.

For the Championship was not turning out to be the Lancia whitewash of previous seasons. The

Martini Integrales, still running in familiar white and striped liveries, after their brief scarlet flirtation, were at full stretch now and Toyota, determined to oust them, invested massively in the World Series. In Greece, with the June Acropolis, the investment finally paid off.

Carlos Sainz, Toyota's Spanish driver, was proving to be a formidable competitor. With Mikael Ericsson in the second Celica GT Four, the Japanese team and their wholly sorted and reliable cars found themselves favourites more often than not. To the relief of all involved in world rallying, the Championship was no longer a foregone conclusion, as Sainz proved in winning a closely fought Acropolis from Kankkunen and, as a result, moving into first place in the Drivers Championship.

In New Zealand, a month later, the Spaniard went even further ahead of Didier Auriol by winning an event which, though still in the World Series calendar, only contributed to the Drivers Championship and not to the World Championship for Rallies, the manufacturers title. This illogical state of affairs, while demonstrating yet again

By winning in Australia towards the end of the 1990 season, Kankkunen virtually assured Lancia of the World Championship once again. It was a close run thing, however, for Toyota now demanded to be taken seriously.

the uncertainties caused by FISA's failure to think through its various seasonal decisions, did allow for a break in the pattern of previous years when the leading manufacturer also always provided the leading driver.

Lancia did not go to New Zealand. There was little commercial benefit to be gained and the rally had no bearing on their Championship position. Argentina, however, was a different matter.

Having successfully competed there for so many years it had become virtually home ground for the Italians and they sent a full complement of three cars. Toyota, meanwhile, made a last minute entry for Carlos Sainz, prompted by his Championship lead and the tactical benefit of having a Spanish speaking driver in the Celica for the South Amercian round. This must have given cause for concern to Lancia. Where previously they had felt largely unchallenged in the Argentine, now they had to cope with a rising star. Even Biasion, with two Argentine wins under his belt, was not sanguine about the anticipated result.

Fortunately for Lancia, Toyota's preparations were rushed and somewhat confused. Sainz, who had not driven the event before, was disadvantaged. Nevertheless he put up a sterling performance right from the start in Buenos Aires and initially he, Biasion and Kankkunen were evenly matched. But as the rally progressed the Toyota's handling grew steadily less certain, causing Sainz to eventually concede the result to Biasion, who had a largely trouble-free rally and beat the Toyota into second place by over 7 minutes.

Argentina, however, was not the happiest of rallies for Lancia. Although Biasion came through largely unscathed, both Kankkunen and Auriol's cars gave cause for future concern. In Kankkunen's case the gearbox failed on Stage 13, leading to his retirement, and for Auriol, who finally finished third, it was a rally characterised by early engine failure and a long subsequent struggle back to the

The 1990 San Remo Rally gave Lancia the World Championship yet again. Auriol beat Kankkunen into first place, but Toyota's Carlos Sainz, who finished third, took the Driver's Championship.

front. A serious accident also affected the team as a whole when one of the large helicopters they were using crashed with 13 people aboard. It exploded in flames and only the greatest good fortune got everyone out without injury.

Good fortune did not accompany Lancia north to Finland in August. The Thousand Lakes Rally saw Japanese cars fill six of the first ten positions and Lancia unable to do better than Kankkunen's fifth place. Carlos Sainz won for Toyota, becoming the first non Finn or Scandinavian ever to do so in the rally's 40 year history. Lancia, even though they still led the Championship for Rallies by 13 points, were struggling.

The indifference which had kept them away from New Zealand did not show itself in the second Antipodean round, the 10th Commonwealth Bank Rally held in Western Australia in the third week of September. With the Championship alive again, the presence of works teams from Toyota, Subaru and Mazda meant that Lancia had to be there to defend their slender lead. Accordingly, Kankkunen, Auriol and Fiorio went to the line in Perth determined to achieve a good result. They were well prepared. Considerable pre-rally testing had been done and Kankkunen, a previous winner, brought with him a good understanding of the special conditions obtaining on the fast, loose surface stages.

In a rally where precise driving was essential the

ABOVE **ECV1 at the Geneva Salon in 1987.**

BELOW **Works Deltas being prepared at Abarth's Corso Marche workshops in Turin. Cars were taken from the production line, stripped and totally rebuilt.**

As assembly progressed the cars began to acquire some of their distinctive livery long before they were anything like complete. They bore a close external resemblance to their road going siblings but underneath virtually nothing was the same.

Finn put up a remarkable and consistently fast performance in winning, beating Sainz back into second place and virtually ensuring Lancia a fourth consecutive World Championship for Rallies.

San Remo, in October, clinched matters for the year. Auriol won from Kankkunen, followed by Sainz into third place and the World Drivers Championship. Honours were even. Lancia had pulled enough out of its ageing Delta to collect the manufacturers prize and Toyota got the GT Four sufficiently together to give their Spanish star pride of place among drivers. Lancia's rally monopoly had been finally broken.

Although as Champions there was now no need to go to Britain for the final round of the 1990 season, Lancia sent cars for Biasion, Kankkunen and

Auriol. It was sensible to do so. Given that the World Championship year was twelve months long, manufacturers and drivers were involved in a virtually seamless activity, with one year rolling unbroken into the next. From a tactical point of view some psychological advantage was to be gained in beginning a new season, not only as Champions, but as victors in the last round of the old year. Lancia, accordingly, took the opportunity to enhance their prestige – or was it just that they were still a little sensitive to the criticism they received for withdrawing from the RAC in '89?

Whatever the reason they made the effort but lost the event. In a rally given great impetus by the introduction of pace notes for the first time, competition between half a dozen works teams and an array of world class drivers was ferocious, fast and relentless, with Kankkunen and Sainz battling it out in front. In the end, luck went the Spaniard's way. On Stage 34, up on the Scottish border and nearing the final stages, Kankkunen suddenly hit unexpected ice, crashed and destroyed the car.

ABOVE **The 1991 World Championship began, as usual, with the Monte Carlo Rally. There were few changes made to the now almost boring successful combination of 16 valve Integrales and team members Biasion, Kankunnen, Auriol, Loubet and Saby. Only Alex Fiorio had gone missing.**

BELOW **Each year, at the start of the season, Lancia invariably send a car or two to the Chamonix Ice Race, a highly specialised 24-hour blind around an increasingly rutted ice rink. Bruno Saby, in suitably polar colours, slides the 16 valve Integrale.**

Sainz was allowed through to victory, the first non-Scandinavian to win since Clark in 1976.

When it came time to tot up the scores in the World Championship for Rallies, the final result was as close as could be. From their seven best scores Lancia had amassed 137 points against Toyota's 131. However, the total score was much closer, there being only a two point gap between them, Lancia collecting more first places, winning six times to Toyota's four and accumulating 164 points altogether.

Such a close finish made it plain that the advan-

Lancia's team for the 1991 season comprised Biasion, Kankkunen, Auriol, Saby and Loubet. For Monte Carlo, the first Championship round of the year, all five drivers appeared. Saby, in Fina colours, finished sixth. Toyota and Sainz won.

tage was shifting firmly to Toyota. Lancia found themselves once more back in their old Fulvia days, when a wonderful car ran out of steam and was overtaken by newcomers. Until the Delta's replacement was made available, the immediate task was to stand their ground against growing competition.

Against this background 1991 began. It was not a time of great change at the Corso Marche. Lombardi remained in charge, assisted by Pianta and Nini Russo. Biasion and Kankkunen were signed again and contracts were issued to Auriol, Loubet and Saby, though the latter two drivers appeared more often in Lancia Fina colours. One important name did go missing however. Alex Fiorio had signed for Ford back in September and, for the first time since 1963, no Fiorio was involved at all with Lancia rallying.

ABOVE **Sainz won again in Portugal but Kankkunen, in car number five, finished in the points despite the odd mishap on the way.**

BELOW **The Integrale now appeared to be showing its age. Kankkunen and his colleagues struggled to finish in the top four in Portugal but none were able to extinguish the rising Japanese star. The Delta's miracle working days seemed over.**

Five 16 valve Integrales contested the first round of the 1991 Championship which began in Monaco on January 24th. Biasion and Kankkunen drove Martini Lancias, Auriol was in a Jolly Club car and Loubet and Saby had Lancia Fina Integrales, with all five able to call on works support. It was a predominently dry rally. Some snow occurred in the highest areas and there were patches of snow and ice on many stages. This created uncertainty over tyre choice, leading the quickest drivers to go for slicks, relying on their stickiness to see them over slippery bits. These conditions did not suit Biasion, who finished second behind Sainz when the rally front runner, French Ford driver Francois Delecour, slowed in the final stages because of suspension damage. Biasion's team mates were seldom in contention, Kankkunen finishing fifth, Saby sixth and Loubet ninth. After years of considering the Monte Carlo their own, Lancia were given further evidence of a changing future.

Since Sweden only counted towards the Drivers Championship, Lancia gave it a miss, although Auriol did turn up looking for personal points. Only marginally more successful than at Monaco, where he retired with engine failure, the Frenchman finished no higher than ninth in a rally dominated by Scandinavians in Japanese cars.

Portugal produced a better outcome, with Lancia's principal drivers finishing in the top four but none quick enough to stop Sainz and the Toyota from claiming 20 points. Not until the Safari in late March did the Integrale reassert itself to give Martini Lancia their first victory of the season, giving Martini a double benefit in the process, since the company was now the principal sponsor of the rally, having taken over from Marlboro, who had supported it for many years.

Nairobi saw three Lancias start and two finish. Kankkunen won, after driving at a pace sufficient to cause Sainz to blow up while, at the same time, conserving the Lancia through another rough and muddy Safari. Jorge Recalde brought his works Integrale into third place but Biasion crashed and retired.

The result put Lancia to within three points of Toyota, who led after four rounds with 57 points. Round five, the Tour de Corse ought to have reversed this position but once again the Toyota of Carlos Sainz proved better on asphalt than Auriol's Fina Integrale. Such was the anticipated pace of the rally that the Lancias were sent out with water cooled brakes, something the company had first tried on the Stratos in the 1970's. But in the high

speed sprint and brake contest Auriol, try as he might, could not overtake Sainz for the lead. The Spaniard drew steadily ahead on the closing stages and Lancia had to be content with an honourable second place.

Thus far in the season Toyota had achieved three first places to Lancia's one. Sainz grew in confidence and stature with each victory, but in the new, closely contested World Championship nothing could be taken for granted. It was therefore no surprise when Lancia reasserted themselves in Greece with a victory by Kankkunen, snatched when Sainz punctured and lost his 21 second lead over the Finn.

The Acropolis also marked a change in team management for Lancia. Fiat's endless game of musical chairs saw Giorgio Pianta replace Lombardi, who moved to Ferrari in place of Fiorio, ousted from Modena after various troubles which included Prost. Pianta, a wily strategist, was well placed to keep Lancia in the points at a time when the dominance of their cars was declining. It would not be easy, however, for at the halfway point in the season Toyota had accumulated 97 points to Lancia's 91 and Sainz led Kankkunen by 77 to 58 points in the Drivers Championship. To stay in the game Lancia needed Toyota to fail completely in rallies which the Italians won. Or, more specifically, they needed Sainz to fail in rallies which they won.

Unfortunately, in Argentina in July, the Spaniard beat them again, evading the might of Lancia to lead home Biasion, Auriol, Kankkunen and Recalde, leaving to them the runner up positions while adding another 20 points to his and Toyota's totals. Ah well!

The Argentine Rally had been formidable. Lancia went into it having won all of the five preceding rallies and had every right to expect a sixth notch on their belt. They certainly went into it well prepared. But Toyota also had ambitions to succeed in front of a Latin crowd and, as a result, both teams, closely matched and with everything to win, put on a memorable performance.

The result was not decided until the last day. The end of the first stage saw Biasion and Sainz equal first and not until the penultimate test did the Spaniard pull ahead to hold his lead through the final stage and win by a mere eight seconds.

Finland and the Thousand Lakes put Lancia back on top of the World Championship by the end of August. Only two cars were sent north, one for Kankkunen and the other for Auriol but this in no way implied a lack of concern on Lancia's part. In

ABOVE **Martini Racing, fighting to retain its supremacy. New team manager Giorgio Pianta was determined to keep the Championship in Turin. From left to right – Pironen, Pianta, Kankkunen, Biasion, Loubet and Petronio.**

BELOW **Lancia reasserted themselves in Greece, with Kankkunen winning the '91 Acropolis Rally from Sainz, who punctured during the final stages. The heyday may have passed but the car was still competing fiercely.**

ABOVE **Kankkunen in Argentina. The fight between Toyota and Lancia was at its closest in the South American rally. Sainz finally won from Biasion by eight seconds. This broke a five rally Lancia winning streak.**

BELOW **Local hero Jorge Recalde put up a good performance in Argentina. The local fans were hard put to decide who to support, since the Spaniard Sainz also offered an appeal to the national spirit.**

fact quite the opposite was the case, for Turin was determined to put all of its resources behind these two in its efforts to prevent Sainz and the Toyota team from scoring more points.

In the event this proved a most difficult task. Despite inadequate notes, Sainz dominated the event, causing Kankkunen to drive at ten tenths whenever possible but without being able to haul in the Spaniard. Not until the final stage of the event did fate reverse the order of things to allow Kankkunen through to first place. Poor Sainz, unable to rely absolutely on pace notes prepared from scratch after his previous year's set had been stolen, overcooked a jump and crashed head first into a ditch. Much damage was done, particularly to the radiator. Temporary repairs were inadequate and he dropped from first to fifth place, allowing Kankkunen to win and Auriol to come second. Lancia took the points, but no one in the team thought they deserved them.

Deserved or not, however, the win restored Lancia's confidence, sending them off to the other end

Thousand Lakes service for Kankkunen's Integrale 16v. The Finn won his home event but only after Sainz, driving with inadequate pace notes, crashed into a ditch and out of contention.

of the world in good heart. Australia's Commonwealth Bank Rally took place between September 20th. and 24th. It was well supported by Mitsubishi, Subaru and Mazda as well as the Championship contenders, Toyota and Lancia. The Italians sent three cars, two new machines for Kankkunen and Auriol and a refettled car for Jorge Recalde. Toyota also provided new cars for Sainz and Schwarz with a refurbished muletto for Australian Neil Bates.

This time it was Sainz who struggled. Having once again been unable to practice at rally speeds, the Spaniard repeatedly overdid things. By day two, having rolled three times in the early stages, he finally put paid to his Toyota and retired, leaving the Lancias in a strong position. Kankkunen was greatly relieved by this, though in some way being first was a mixed blessing since it required him to plough a way through the notoriously loose and slippery pebbles that made up much of the road. Still, it was better than eating Japanese dust. For a while, during the third day, Auriol gave him a break by moving ahead to take a turn at sweeping, but towards the close suffered engine failure and retired.

The final day saw Kankkunen retain his lead but suffer pressure from Kenneth Eriksson in the Mitsubishi VR4. Not that this unsettled the Lancia driver. The prospect of two wins in a row was sufficient to keep him ahead to the finish and to earn enough points for the Italian team to stay on top of the Championship – though only just.

Toyota's last chance of staying in the game now lay in San Remo, Lancias's home ground. It was a slim chance; with five works Integrales lined up against them and the fervent tifosi lined up at the roadside, Sainz and Schwarz, in the two lone Celica GT4's, were as Christians amongst lions. To make matters worse, one of the Christians was wounded, for Sainz was still suffering the effect of his Australian crashes when he went to the start in San Remo on Sunday, October 13th at 9.30 in the morning. Exactly four days later he was back, in sixth place with four of the five Lancias ranged

Kankkunen on a night stage during the New Zealand Rally.

above him and the World Championship for Rallies going, yet again, to the Turin team. It was their fifth Championship in the five years since Group A superseded the formidable but disgraced Group B; it was also their fifth Championship with the same car, which left all of their competitors wondering how on earth they managed to do so with the venerable but unbeatable Delta.

With the World Championship secure, attention now turned to the Drivers Championship. Victory at San Remo had gone to Didier Auriol in a Jolly Club/Fina Integrale. Kankkunen, Lancia Martini's number one had hit a rock during the second stage of the rally and been forced to retire. As a consequence of this misfortune he was the only works driver not to finish the event, an error paid for in Driver Championship points. To compensate for this it was necessary to make a journey to Spain, in mid November, in an attempt to close up on Carlos Sainz, who led the Finnish driver by eight points after the Italian event.

Going to Spain was something of a role reversal for the Lancia driver who, despite the company of Jolly Club drivers Andrea Aghini and Gustavo Trelles, now played Christian to the Sainz lion. Fortunately, the lion blew it, retiring on stage eight with engine failure and allowing Kankkunen through to take second place to Toyota's number two, Armin Schwarz. This gave him sufficient points to move ahead of Sainz to the top of the table. The matter now awaited resolution in

Britain, in eleven days time.

Nothing is ever predictable in the RAC. If something can go wrong, it will, particularly on the fast, slippery forest stages. This leads teams to provide themselves with adequate back up, not only in terms of service crews but also in having a number of cars in the team. This time, however, certainly for Lancia and Toyota, only one car in each team counted, for the event would be hand-to-hand combat between Kankkunen and Sainz. The Japanese therefore sent one car, unlike Lancia, belt and braces Lancia, who sent four: Martini cars for Kankkunen and Biasion and Jolly club machines for Auriol and Saby. In many ways it seemed unnecessarily expensive, but actually was wholly in keeping with Lancia's historic unpredictability where the RAC was concerned; sometimes they ignored it, other times they swamped it, seeming to regard it now with affection, now with loathing . In 1991 the RAC received their full attention.

Kankkunen undoubtedly found such whole

ABOVE **Auriol takes one of the Fina Lancias through an RAC water splash.**

BELOW **Kankkunen on a forest stage during the same event. The showdown with Sainz was effectively over when the Spaniard crashed his Toyota in the Redesdale Forest.**

This special cabriolet is one of two built by Lancia for the Agnelli family. It is based on the 16 valve Integrale Evoluzione and is one of the few special bodied Deltas to have been produced. The final batch of Evoluzione Integrales consisted of 2000 cars built at the Chivasso factory before it closed. The cars, fitted with CATs, were built under the supervision of the coachbuilder Maggiora.

hearted support most encouraging. By contrast, Sainz must have felt quite alone, despite the presence of Mark Duez in a Toyota Fina car. Still, in a one to one contest, it was all down to him and to Kankkunen.

The first serious part of the rally was the second Etape in Wales, on day two. Here Sainz and Auriol made the running, with Kankkunen taking care not to do anything silly. All would have been well had his team mate, Miki Biasion, driving his last rally for Lancia before joining Ford, also taken care, for on Stage 21, in Clocaenog, he rolled massively, destroying the car but escaping unhurt.

Next day, with the rally moved north to the Lakes and the Scottish border, Auriol, Sainz and

Kankkunen all remained in contention. The lead changed hands from time to time but in the Redesdale Forest Sainz crashed, doing damage to his car and ultimately sealing his fate, for on subsequent stages the Toyota was seen to be down on power. The cause, not necessarily connected with the crash but not improved by it, was a faulty head gasket which the Toyota mechanics were forced to fix at the roadside.

After that it was all over. Kankkunen, steadily extending his lead to leave Sainz trailing in third place, became World Rally Champion for the third time and Lancia achieved yet another Grand Slam.

But then, as if suddenly tired of the whole endless, expensive roundabout of rallying, the Italians gave up. In December, shortly before Christmas, Lancia announced their withdrawal from World Championship rallying. After twenty six years in the limelight, the game palled: the latest HF Integrale evolution was handed over to a new team, Martini Racing, and what was still, at heart, Squadra Lancia, was wound up. History repeated itself.

Despite their sudden, generally unexpected abandonment of the one area of motorsport in which Italian cars were successful, Lancia's

Zagato Hyena Integrale prototype. This belated addition to the Delta range came about through the interest of the Dutch company, Lusso Service. Coming so late in the Integrale's production cycle Lancia, with good reason, felt unable to support the venture. Lusso therefore buy cars from an Italian dealer, strip them in Holland and then return them to Italy and Zagato before ultimately receiving them back for sale.
Commedia dell'arte.

decision to retire was perhaps less surprising to those with knowledge of their position. The Fiat empire was, and is, in some difficulty. With an overall decline in European car sales, the vast sums of cash needed to support a winning World Rally team were less readily available than previously. And anyway, with Martini (also a Fiat property) ready to sponsor the latest evolution cars in the 1992 season and the experienced Jolly Club organisation available to prepare and manage them, Lancia were hardly denying themselves very much in giving up direct responsibility for the onerous task of running their old and boringly successful Delta. It was, perhaps, more a change of form than substance.

The final evolution of the Delta, that restrained little box introduced back in 1979, was the Book of Revelations to Giugiaro's Genesis. It was publicly launched in early October, 1991 and a couple of months later, when *Car*'s Richard Bremner tested it against Porche's Carrera 4 and Lotus's Elan SE, that writer pronounced it the best point-to-pointer you could buy. What it could do for Kankkunen it could do for you – and all for a mere £22,940.

Lancia's engineers had finally produced the apogee of the road going 4X4. External changes, though subtle, were immediately obvious; the new car wore a slender tailgate spoiler, new front light clusters, new 15 x 7.5" alloy wheels and a redesigned bonnet and bulges. It still looked like Adam, but only just.

Underneath, it gained better suspension, steering (with an oil cooler for the power assistance!) and brakes to cope with the power increase, raised to 210bhp at 5750rpm but nullified, in terms of extra performance, by a corresponding increase in weight. Ah, the consequence of age!

There is now little more to say of the Delta as we

know it; Lancia's duck never became a swan but turned instead into a very powerful goose. When it was introduced, many dismissed the car as merely a Fiat; now, at the end of its life, the final evolution has become the latest version of the last 'proper Lancia', that old canard so often heard flapping around the via Vincenzo Lancia! Whether or not such pessimism finally turns out to be true this time depends on forces beyond the control of Lancia, and possibly beyond the control of Fiat. The Delta's replacement is well advanced. The name will continue but the beast will be different and somewhere at the via Vincenzo Lancia there may be other more radical machines being planned, one of which might, in time, become the next example of the 'last proper Lancia'. Who knows, other than the Japanese, perhaps?

The Delta, the unbeatable box, has its place in history. An unlikely candidate for posterity at the beginning if its life, spawning few pretty offspring other than Pininfarina's aptly named HIT (a modest acronym derived from High Italian Technology) and one or two speculations from Giugiaro himself and latterly from Zagato in the form of the grotesquely named Hyena, it became memorable through sheer persistence. Initially self-effacing, the dramatic circumstances in World Rallying saved it from oblivion: in the hands of a group of engineers and drivers inspired by one of the great tacticians of motorsport, Cesare Fiorio, it emerged as Lancia's longest-running ever production vehicle and to date (and certainly for the foreseeable future) has won more World Championships than any other rally car. The Delta has earned its right to be remembered and yes, perhaps it will be the last real Lancia after all.

Technical Specifications

DELTA AND PRISMA, (TYPE ZLA 831)

Delta and Prisma 1300

engine type	831.A.000 or 831.B.000
bore × stroke	86.4 × 55.5/55.4 mm
capacity	1301 cc/1299 cc
compression ratio	9.1:1
from 1983	9.5:1
construction	four cyl, in line with belt driven sohc.transversely mounted
max. bhp	75 @ 5800 rpm
from 1983	78 @ 5800 rpm
max. torque kgfm	10.7 @ 3500 rpm
carburettor	1 Weber 32 DAT 7
transmission	s.d.p. clutch and fully synchronised gearbox; f.w.d.
gear ratios (:1)	3.583/2.235/1.454/1.042/ R.3.714 (4 sp)
up to 1983	3.583/2.235/1.550/1.163/ 0.959/R.3.714
from 1983	3.583/2.235/1.454/1.042/ 0.863/R.3.714
from 1986	4.091/2.235/1.469/1.043/ 0.863/R.3.714
final drive (:1)	3.756
front suspension	ind. with McPherson-type struts.
rear suspension	ind. with twin-parallel lower transverse suspension arms., longitudinal reaction arms, coil-spring struts.
steering	rack and pinion-type, with optional pwr.ass.
brakes	hydr. op. and vacuum ass. dual split brake system with front discs and rear drums
wheel size	5B–13
tyre size	145 SR–13 (Delta 4–speed model) or 165/70 SR–13
wheelbase	2475 mm
track front/rear	1400/1400 mm
lgth × wth × ht	3890 × 1620 × 1380 mm
Prisma	4180 × 1620 × 1385 mm
weight	935–955 kg
top speed	155 km/h

Delta and Prisma 1500

All specifications as for Delta/Prisma 1300 except:

engine type	831.A1.000 or 831.B1.000
bore × stroke	86.4 × 63.9 mm
capacity	1498 cc
compression ratio	9.2:1
from 1986	9.5:1
max. bhp	85 @ 5800 rpm
from 1986	80 @ 5600 rpm
max. torque kgfm	12.5 @ 3500 rpm
from 1986	12.5 @ 3200 rpm
carburettor	Weber 32 DAT 8
from 1986	Weber 32/34 TLDA 2
transmission	hydraulic torque converter and 3–speed aut, transmission optional
gear ratios, manual (:1)	3.583/2.235/1.55/1.163/ 0.959/R.3.714
automatic	2.346/1.402/1.0/R.2.346
final drive (:1), aut.	3.595
weight	940–975 kg
top speed	160 km/h
(automatic)	155 km/h

Delta 1100 (Greece only)

All specifications as for Delta 1300 except:

engine type	831.B8.000
bore × stroke	80 × 55.5 mm
capacity	1116 cc
max. bhp	64 @ 6000 rpm
max. torque kgfm	8.6 @ 3000 rpm
top speed	140 km/h

Delta 1600 GT and Prisma 1600

All specifications as for Delta and Prisma 1300 except:

engine type	831.A4.000 or 831.B6.000
bore × stroke	84 × 71.5 mm
capacity	1585 cc
compression ratio	9.7:1
construction	four cyl. in line with belt-driven dohc
max. bhp	105 @ 5800 rpm
from 1986	100 @ 5900 rpm
max. torque kgfm	13.8 @ 3500 rpm
carburettor	1 Weber 34 DAT 16
gear ratios (: l)	3.853/2.235/1.55/1.163/ 0.959/R.3.714

final drive (:1), aut.	3.588
brakes	discs front and rear
wheel size	5.5 J–14
tyre size	165/65 SR–14
weight	975–990 kg
top speed	180 km/h/p

Delta 1600 Grle and Prisma 1600 ie

All specifications as for Delta and Prisma 1600 except:

engine type	831.B7.000
max. bhp	108 @ 5900 rpm
with cat.	90 @ 6250 rpm
max. torque kgfm	13.8 @ 3500 rpm
with cat.	12.5 @ 4250 rpm
injection	Weber l.A.W. electronic fuel injection
gear ratios (: l)	3.545/2.267/1.541 / 1.156/0.967/R.3.909
final drive (:1)	3.588
with cat.	3.562
weight	995–1020 kg
top speed	185 km/h
with cat.	175 m/h.

Delta 1600 HF and HF ie

All specifications as for Delta 1600GT except:

engine type	831.B3.000
construction	additional turbocharging
compression ratio	8.0:1
with cat	7.5:1
max. bhp UP TO 1986	130 @ 5600 rpm
from 1986	140 @ 5500 rpm
from 1986 with cat.	132 @ 5500 rpm
max. torque kgfm	
up to 1986	19.5 @ 3700 rpm
from 1986	21 @ 3750 rpm (with over boost)
from 1986 with cat.	20 kgfm @ 2750 rpm
carburettor up to 1986	1 Weber 32 DAT 18 with Garrett T3 turbocharger and intercooler
injection from 1986	Weber lAW electronic injection with Garrett T3 turbo and intercooler
gear ratios (:1)	
up to 1986	3.583/2.235/1.542/1.154 0.903/R.3.667
from 1986	3.545/2.267/1.541/1.156 0.891 /R3.909
final drive (:1)	
up to 1986	3.4
from 1986	3.353
from 1986 with cat.	3.167
wheel size, up to 1986	135 TR 340
from 1986	5.5 J–14
tyre size up to 1986	170/65R 340 (Michelin TRX)
from 1986	165/65 HR–14
weight	1000–1060 kg
top speed up to 1986	195 km/h
from 1986	203 km/h
from 1986 with cat.	198 km/h

Prisma ds

All specifications as for Prisma 1600 except:

engine type	831.D.000
bore × stroke	82.6 × 90 mm
capacity	1929 cc
compression ratio	21:1
construction	four cyl, in line with belt driven sohc and indirect fuel injection
max. bhp	65 @ 4600 rpm
max. torque kgfm	12.1 @ 2000 rpm
injection	Bosch VE diesel injection system
gear ratios (: l)	4.09/2.235/1.469/1.043/ 0.827/R.3.714
final drive (: l)	3.588
wheel size	SB–13
tyre size	165/70 SR–13
weight	1015 kg
top speed	158 km/h

Delta and Prisma turbo ds

All specifications as for Prisma ds except:

engine type	831.D1.000
compression ratio	20:1
construction	additional turbocharging
max. bhp	80 @ 4200 rpm
max. torque kgfm	17.5 @ 2400 rpm
injection	Bosch VE diesel injection system with KKK turbocharger and intercooler
gear ratios (: l)	3.583/2.235/1.524/1 154/0.838/R.3.667
final drive (:1)	3.048
wheel size	5.5 J–14
tyre size	165/65 SR–14
weight	1045 kg
top speed	170 km/h

Prisma 4WD

All specifications as for Prisma 1600 and Delta 1600 except:

engine type	831.B4/000
bore × stroke	84 × 90 mm
capacity	1995 cc
compression ratio	9.7:1
max. bhp	115 @ 5400 rpm
with cat.	112 @ 5500 rpm
max. torque kgfm	16.6 @ 3250 rpm
with cat.	16 @ 4000 rpm
injection	Weber lAW electronic fuel injection
transmission	permanent 4WD with viscous central differential. Individual engagement for rear lim. slip diff.
gear ratios (: l)	3.750/2.235/1.518/1.132/ 0.928/R.3.583
final drive (:1)	3.421
torque split	56% front, 44% rear
steering	power assisted rack and pinion
tyre size	185/60 HR–14
brakes	larger diameter ventilated front discs
track front/rear	141/140.5 cm
weight	1180–1220 kg
top speed	184 km/h
with cat.	181 km/h

Delta 4WD and Group A

All specifications as for Prisma 4WD except:

engine type	831.B5.000
compression ratio	8.0:1 (Gr. A:7.5)

max. bhp	165 @ 5250 rpm
with cat.	150 @
Group A	260 @ 6250 rpm
max. torque kgfm	29 @ 2750 rpm with over boost
Group A	38 @ 3000 rpm
injection	Weber lAW el. fuel inj. with Garrett T3 turbocharger and intercooler
transmission	permanent 4wd with automatic Torsen rear lim. slip diff.
Group A	additional front lim. slip diff.
gear ratios (: l)	3.50/2.235/1.518/1.132/ 0.928/R.3.583
final drive (: l)	2.944
brakes Group A	ventilated 280 mm discs
wheel size	5.5 J–14
Group A	7 J–15
tyre size	185/60 HR–14
Group A	210/580–15
wheelbase	2480 mm
track front & rear	
Group A	1340/1440 cm
weight	1190 kg
top speed	208km/h

Delta Integrale and Group A
All specifications as for Delta 4WD except:

engine type	831.C5.000
max. bhp	185 @ 5300 rpm
Group A	280 @ 6500 rpm
max. torque kgfm	31– 3500 rpm
Group A	39 @ 4000 rpm
transmission Group A	non synchronised 6–speed
final drive (: l)	3.111
brakes	larger diameter ventilated front discs
wheel size	6J–15, light alloy
Group A	9–16
tyre size	195/55 VR–15
Group A	24/61–16 (Michelin)
track front/rear	1425/1405 mm
Group A	1488/1458 mm
lgth × wth × ht	3900 × 1685 × 1360 mm
weight	1215 kg
Group A	1120 kg
top speed	215 km/h

Delta Integrale 16V and Group A
All specifications as for Delta Integrale except:

engine type	831.D5.000
construction	turbo charged four cyl, in line with belt drivendohc and four valves per cylinder.
max. bhp	200 @ 5500 rpm
Group A	295@ 7000 rpm
max. torque kgfm	31 @ 3000 rpm
Group A	41 @ 4500 rpm
torque split	43% front, 57% rear
weight	1250 kg
Group A	1100 kg
top speed	215 km/h

Delta Integrale 16 V Evoluzione
All specifications as for Delta Integrale 16V except:

max. bhp	210 @ 5750 rpm
max. torque kgfm	31 @ 3500 rpm ·
track front/rear	1502/1500 mm

width	1700 mm
weight	1300kg
top speed	220km/h

Note: for markets with stricter emission rules, the 16V engine was excluded. Instead a 180 bhp and 30 kgfm eight-valve version was available, with three-way catalyst for the Integrale, Integrale 16V and Integrale 16V Evoluzione.

Delta S4 and Group B

type	038 ARO
engine type	233 ATR 185
bore × stroke	88.5 × 71.5 mm
capacity	1759 cc
compression ratio	7.8:1 (Gr. B 7.0)
construction	midship mounted four cyl. in line with belt-driven dohc and four valves per cyl. Combined supercharging and turbocharging.
max. bhp	250 @ 6750 rpm
Group B	480 @ 8400 rpm
max. torque kgfm	29 @ 4500 rpm
Group B	45 @ 5000 rpm
injection	Weber lAW electronic fuel injection with Roots-type positive displacement blower and KKK exhaust-driven turbocharger and twin intercoolers
transmission	fully synchronised ZF 5 speed gearbox and permanent 4WD with central and rear limited slip diffs.
Group B	Hewland gearbox internals and additional front limited slip differential
torque split	30% front, 70% rear
Group B	var. between 25/75% and 40/60%
primary gear red. (:1)	1.905
gear ratios (: l)	2.50/1.579/1.115/0.862/ 0.710/R.2.462
final drive (: l)	2.643
front suspension	ind. with twin parallel w'bones, coil springs and anti-roll bar
rear suspension	ind. with twin-parallel w'bones, twin coil springs per wheel and anti-roll bar
steering	rack and pinion-type, with pneumatic ass.
brakes	vacuum assisted four wheel disc brakes of 30cm diameter
wheel size	8J–16 light-alloy
Group B	8J–16 front, 12J–16 rear
tyre size	205/55 VR–16
Group B	230/45 VR–16 front, 290/60 VR–16 rear
wheelbase	2440 mm
track front/rear	1500/1520 mm
Group B	1510/1535 mm
lgth × wth × ht	4004 × 1800 × 1250 mm
weight	1200 kg
Group B	960 kg
top speed	225 km/h

Index

Ericsson, Mikael 67, 78–9, 83, *102*, 103, *104*, 105, 108, *108*, 127–39, *128*, *135*, 148, 156–7, *156*, 161
Eriksson, Kenneth 111, 157

Falchetto, Battista 8
Fauchille 111
Ferguson differentials 55, 56, 85, *95*, 97, 133
Ferrari 7, 10, 20, 33, 151
Fiat 7–8, 10, 11, 13, 15–16, 20, 45, 48, 77
Fiat 128 25
Fiat 130 Coupe 16
Fiat 508 Millemiglia 8
Fiat 600 48
Fiat Auto 20
Fiat Panda 26, 42
Fiat Ritmo *11*, 13, 14, 25
Fiat Strada *11*, 13, 22
Fiat Strato 14
Fiat VSS 142
Fiat Zagato 10, 48
FID cylinder heads 142
Fiorio, Alessandro 99, 117, 127, *129*, 130, *132*, 135–9, *135*, 141, 156, 161, 175
Fiorio, Cesare 31, *48*, 49–57, *64*, 69, 77–8, 84–5, 93–5, 99–101, *104*, *108*, 113, 117, 148, 151, 158, *159*, *163*, 185
FISA *49*, 70, 73, 76, 78, 83, 85, 99, 102, 108, 117, *121*, 125, 148, 166
Ford 55, 95, 111, 119, 127, 132, 133, 148
four wheel drive 25–6, 27, 42, *43*, *47*, 51, 54–6, *72*
  see also Lancia Delta HF 4WD, Lancia Integrale
France 20
Frankfurt Motor Show *18*, 19, 98, 121

Garrett turbochargers 26, 34, 93, 99, 100, 121, *122*, 133
Garrone, Felice 147
gearboxes 15, 25
Germany 20
Ghia 10, 19
Ghidella, Vittoria 28
Giacosa, Dante 8
Giugiaro, Giorgetto *7*, 8, 11, *12*, 13, 14, *15*, 16, 18, 19, 28, *28*, *37*, *92*, *125*
Gobbato, Pier Ugo 14
Grundel, Kalle 79, 83

Heron Group 29

Hewland/Lancia gearboxes 55
HF Squadra Corse 69
Holland 20
homologation regulations 49, *49*, 51, 56–7, 98–9, 102, *123*, 125, 148

Ice School, Sestriere 112
interior design *40*, *41*, 42, 44, *48*, *123*
Isemburg, Conny 112
Ital Design 11, *12*, *16*, 26
Ital Styling 19
Italian National Championship 77
Italian National Rally School 112
Ivory Coast Rally 161

Japan 117, 158
Jaray, P 8
Jolly Club 99, 127, 130, 148, 151, 161, 181

Kankkunen, Juha 67, 73, 77–9, 83, *83*, 99–108, *101*, *103*, *105–6*, *108*, 111–19, *113*, 139, 148, *150*, 157, *160*, 161, *162*, 169, *169*, *171*, 173–85
Kevlar propeller shafts 133
Kirkland, Mike *131*, 138, 151
Kivimaki 56, 70
KKK turbos 34, 99, 100

La Mandria track 26
Lafitte, Jacques 133
Lampredi, Aurelio 30, 33–4, *46*, 48, 51
Lancar 29
Lancia, Gianni 49
Lancia, Vincenzo 14, 29
Lancia Appia 13
Lancia Aprilia 8, 10–11, 13
Lancia Ardea 13
Lancia Augusta 13
Lancia B20 10
Lancia Beta 11, 13
Lancia Delta ECV1 142, *143*, 144, *144*, *172*
Lancia Delta ECV2 142, 144, 146–7, *146–7*
Lancia Delta GTie 88, *90*
Lancia Delta HF 4WD 84–5, *85–96*, 88, 93, 95, 97–9, *98*, 100–3, *100–10*, 105, 108, 111–13, *112–16*, 115–19, *118*
Lancia Fulvia 10–11, 13, 31, 77
Lancia Gamma 7, 8, 11, 13
Lancia HF Delta 33, *35*, *71*, *72*
Lancia Integrale 42, *60*, *91*,

120–85, *120–37*, *139–40*, *149–55*, *159–76*, *178–84*
Lancia Lambda 8
Lancia Prisma 30, *35–7*, *41*, 42, *43*, 44
Lancia Prisma 4WD 85, *85*, 88, 93
Lancia Rally Abarth 33, 49, 51
Lancia S4 Delta 45, *45–50*, 48–9, 51–2, *53–5*, 54–7, *57–9*, 59, 75, *76*
Lancia S4 Stradale *53*, 54
Lancia Stratos 7, 8, 27, 51, 56, 77
Lancia Thema 42
Lane, Eric 102
Limone, Sergio 51, 111
liveries *80–1*, 97, *152*, 158, 170
Loewy, Raymond 10
Lombard 60, 161
Lombardi, Claudio 46, 52, 56, 69, 84, 93, 95, 97, 103, 111, *123*, 130, 133, 142, 147, 151, 154
Loubet, Yves *107*, 111–12, 127, 130, 135–9
LX model 24, 25, *29*

McCarthy, Mike 40
McPherson struts 14–15, 22, 27
Magnetti Marelli Microplex system 38–9, *39*
maintenance 42, 56
Manufacturers Championship 116
Marlboro Rally (Argentina) 117
Martini Lancia liveries *80–1*, 97, 158, 169–70
Maserati 10, 11
Mazda 95, 102, *102*, 105, 108, 111, 117, 119, 127, 139, 148, 180
Messori, Pier Paolo 51, 56
Michelin tyres 40, *122*, 130, 132, 158
Michelotti 8
Mikkola, Hannu 62, 64, 111, 127
Milan Grand Prix 45
Mille Pistes (France) 57
Mitsubishi 125, 148, 157, 180
Monte Carlo Rally (France) 70–1, 98, 100–2, *100–1*, 127, 130, 148, *149*, 161, 165–6, 174
Mortinho, Joaquim 75
Motor 24, 117
Motor Sport 100–1, 117
Munari, Sandro 137

New Zealand Rally 78, 79, *116*, 117, 156, 171